MAKING
NEW TESTAMENT
TOYS

MARGARET HUTCHINGS

with illustrations by
the author

MILLS & BOON LIMITED
LONDON

TAPLINGER
PUBLISHING COMPANY
NEW YORK

Other books by the same author
The "What Shall I Do?" series
Making Old-Testament Toys
Modern Soft Toy Making, etc.

First published in Great Britain in 1972 by
Mills & Boon Limited, 17–19 Foley Street,
London W1A 1DR

First published in the United States in 1972 by
Taplinger Publishing Company, New York

British ISBN 0–263–05206–0

American ISBN 0-8008-5078-5

Library of Congress Catalog Card Number
72-2185

Set on Monophoto '600' and made and printed in
Great Britain by Thomson Litho, East Kilbride,
Scotland

Contents

4

Katie Jane has just arrived! This little book has been waiting for her and is dedicated with love and as a welcome to my newest Grand-daughter.

Foreword

When some time ago I started work on designs for a book of toys based on biblical themes, I started in the usual place " . . . in the beginning . . ." As I worked on, the scope seemed absolutely endless and many frustrating days were spent trying to decide just what to include and what to leave out!

Eventually the book was split in two and some of you will already have met *Making Old Testament Toys*. Here is the second half which as with every book I write has been a great joy to prepare. Like its companion it is planned for use by all age groups, none of the work is complicated and a great deal can be done by the very young. I have tried to include as much variety as possible so that boys and girls, mothers and teachers, young and old can work together—some sticking, some stitching, some cutting, some painting, some winding, some knitting, and their combined efforts will form the many groups and sets within these covers.

As the vicar of my own parish so aptly remarked "The Old Testament can be 'fun' but the New Testament has something 'special' about it." I have tried to keep that "special" feeling yet to create toys and games which will help to sort out the many stories and characters, thus helping to bring them to life—I can only hope I have succeeded.

M.H.

GENERAL INSTRUCTIONS AND SOME SUGGESTIONS TO HELP YOU

1. All references are taken from the Revised Version of the Bible.

2. Always read right through the instructions given for the toy or model you have decided to make before starting work. Make sure you understand them and that you have all the necessary "bits and pieces" available.

3. Trace the patterns on to thin cardboard and cut out a series of templates (pattern shapes) so that you can draw round them on the material. This makes for quick and accurate cutting out and the templates can be stored in sets for future use.

4. Refer constantly to the main picture of each toy you make, but do not be afraid to branch out and experiment. Part of the charm of this sort of work is that no two people ever work in quite the same way and consequently no two creatures or characters ever look *exactly* the same.

5. Flesh pink or fawn felt will do equally well for the skin of your characters and almost any colours for their clothes (although rich people often wore purple)—so use what you have by you. The main thing to remember is that they did not wear spotted or flowered tunics and that coarsely-woven materials look more authentic.

6. You will need lots of matchboxes, Sifta Salt containers (cone-shaped), cardboard tubes, lolly (popsicle) sticks, wooden ice cream spoons, tops of discarded tights, beads, sequins, vegetable nets, scraps of wood and felt and gold card from various boxes and packages, so start a "bit box" and collect these oddments in it. Your friends will help, I'm sure!

7. Where pipe cleaners of a specific colour are mentioned, white ones may easily be painted with poster paints or coloured inks. Alternatively packets of assorted colours may be purchased from many craft shops. Brown hair curlers from Woolworths or large stores are useful—and exactly like pipe cleaners.

NOTE TO AMERICAN READERS

Short descriptions are supplied below for a few terms that may be unfamiliar to American readers of this book:

Sifta Salt container: This is a conical, flat-topped shape about 8 inches high. An equivalent can be made from cardboard, following the drawing on page 8.

Bobble fringing: Decorative fringe trimming to sew on edges.

Dolly peg: Old-fashioned clothes pin. An alternative is shown in text (page 22).

Smartie tube: Small tube of cardboard. As substitute, make a roll of cardboard about big enough to slip over your forefinger.

Adhesive: A rubber-based one was used for the original toys, but a strong all-purpose glue such as Elmer's Glue-all may be substituted.

Oddments: Remnants.

Instructions for all nativity figures

"And they came with haste and found Mary and Joseph and the babe lying in a manger."

(St. Luke 2.16)

This simply made set of Nativity figures, forming a Christmas crib, would be a delightful group project— a whole family, class or club combining to collect the necessary "pieces" and put them together. The figures are easily made and designed so that you can add more characters or make less, just as you wish. You will find that some of the animals in the companion volume on the Old Testament, such as the camel, the ass and the sheep and goat, will fit particularly well into this group and you might like to add the little ox on page 63 of this volume.

N.B. Patterns for a much more detailed set of wired Nativity figures suitable for a skilled needlewoman appear in *Dolls and How to Make Them*.

TO MAKE THE WHOLE SET YOU WILL NEED

Seven Sifta Salt containers for bodies. Eighteen lolly (popsicle) sticks for manger and hands. Four wooden ice cream spoons for hands. One empty cotton spool, one matchbox, and a jar lid for "gifts". Wire for crooks. One wooden bead for the Baby's

head. Bandage for his clothes. Silver or gold cardboard, silver foil, beads, sequins: for halos and decoration. Grey and yellow wool, black bobble fringing, and a little cotton wool for hair. Several packets of pipe cleaners for fur trimming. Tops of old nylon tights for heads, felt to match for hands. Yellow, brown and flesh pink stockinette (or other soft stretchy material) for heads and felt to match for hands. Tissue paper and kapok or similar for stuffing.

N.B. The Sifta Salt containers which are conical shaped may be substituted by straight containers such as scouring powder tins, but these will not look so attractive; or cone-shaped bases may be made from thin cardboard.

Of the originals many were covered with felt, but if you do not possess oddments of this material you may prefer to use up scraps of something else. Silks, cottons, velvets may all be used for the clothes and the edges either left raw or tiny hems taken according to how permanent you want the figures to be. The ideas given here are basic so that you can adapt them to suit yourself. Should you decide to buy felt for the clothes, read through the instructions for the figure concerned making sure of exactly what is needed, then take the containers and any necessary patterns with you to the shop in order to buy it in the most economical way.

GENERAL INSTRUCTIONS FOR ALL FIGURES.

IT IS IMPORTANT TO READ THROUGH THESE CAREFULLY BEFORE STARTING WORK AND TO REFER BACK TO THEM CONSTANTLY.

1. *Heads:* Make as shown for the Devil, page 40 and Fig. 15, using

the type of material and colour suggested for each figure. Size is given in each case. When adding hair, etc., always have gathers at the back where they are hidden.

2. *Bodies:* Salt drums may be covered as shown in Fig. 1A, i.e. a circle at base and top and a strip round the sides all oversewn in place. Alternatively, the felt may be stuck to the container as shown for the Apostles, page 30 No. 2, and Fig. 9. Yet again you could have a circle at the base and a strip round the sides which is about $\frac{3}{4}$ in. (2 cm.) too tall, gather all round this, pull up tightly and fasten off at centre top of

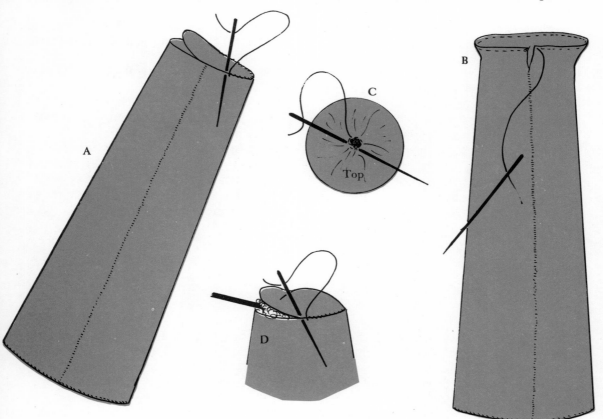

Fig. 1   Covering salt drums for the Nativity Figures.

drum (Fig. 1B and C). If a thin material is substituted for felt the base may be gathered up in a similar way and the circles omitted altogether.

N.B. A little cotton wool under the top circle (Fig. 1 D) helps to pad out the "hollow" top of the container making it easier to stitch the heads in position.

3. *Shorten Salt Drums* for the kneeling figures with a pen knife. Always cut the surplus lengths from the *bottom* of the container. It will not matter that these figures have no solid base, the felt alone will suffice, but fill them tightly with crumpled paper to avoid crushing.

4. *Arms:* Cover lolly (popsicle) sticks or wooden ice cream spoons with felt as given for the Dog's legs, page 25 No. 4 and Fig. 7. Or by placing between two pieces of felt,

stab stitching round outline of wood, then cutting and trimming felt to fit (Fig. 2, A and B). Note the length and colour in each case. Cut sticks with old scissors or a penknife.

5. *Assembling Parts:* Stitch heads and arms securely to bodies, using strong thread and ladder stitch, i.e. one stitch alternately on head or limb and body.

6. *Features:* Draw these with felt tip or ballpoint pens.

7. *For Firm Standing of Kneeling Figures:* Arrange their "folds of robes" on the table, then place each figure on a sheet of thin cardboard smeared with Copydex or Glue-all. Press figure down, then cut cardboard away all round edge of "train", or robe and front curved edge of salt container, so that it does not show, but makes a flat, firm base.

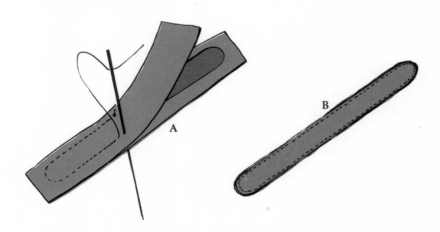

Fig. 2   Covering lolly sticks for arms.

JOSEPH

". . . Joseph . . . was of the house and lineage of David . . ." (St. Luke 2.4)

HOW TO MAKE HIM (Read the instructions on page 7)

Use brown felt.

1. Cut out sleeves and fold of robe to broken line (patterns pages 89 and 90) and a strip of brown felt 6¼ × 2½ inches (13·5 cm × 6·5 cm), for his cowl. Four pieces.

2. *Body:* Shorten a salt container to 6 inches (15 cm) and cover with felt. (Fig. 1 A or B).

3. *Arms:* Cut a lolly (popsicle) stick into two and cover with fawn felt. (Fig. 2).

4. *Head:* Using top of old nylon tights make a ball about 1½ inches (4 cm) diameter. (See page 8). Draw black eyes, red nose. Stick scraps of grey wool in place for brows.

5. *Hair and Beard:* Sew thick bundles of grey wool to top of head for hair and under nose for beard. Arrange carefully and stick in place. Trim to shape.

6. *Assembling:* Sew head to front edge of top of body, leaning forwards a little, and sew arms to sides, arranging them to meet at one side instead of centre front.

7. *Sleeves:* On each arm tuck the side A—B over arm and down "inside" (A to the front) then stick to robe along A—B. Bring the sleeve over arm and stick or stitch to robe along D—C and at centre back of robe C—B—the sleeve will have a draped effect.

8. *Cowl:* Take a large pleat in each of the two short ends and secure with a few stitches. Stitch in place—short ends in front just under beard, and stitch at centre back on lower edge. Stitch "fold of robe" in place as given for Mary, page 13, No. 8.

9. *Halo:* Using the pattern for Angel No. 1, page 95, cut a circle in gold or silver cardboard or cover white cardboard with foil. Stick in place.

10. *Staff and Girdle:* Knot a length of string round waist for girdle and make a staff from a rough twig, stitching in place between hands or to robe, also at base.

" . . . Joseph and (the baby's) mother marvelled at those things which were spoken of Him . . ."

(St. Luke 2.33)

MARY

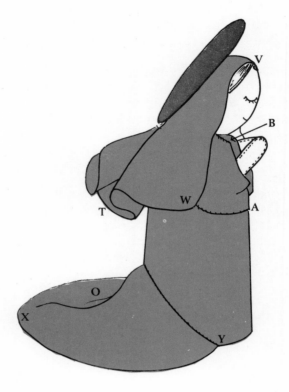

" . . . for behold from henceforth all generations shall call me blessed."
(St. Luke 1.48)

HOW TO MAKE HER (Read the instructions on page 7).

Use soft blue felt.

1. Cut out sleeves, veil (to solid line) and fold of robe (to broken line), patterns pages 89 and 90. Four pieces.

2. *Body:* Shorten a salt container to 4½ inches (11·5 cm) and cover with soft blue felt. (Fig. 1 A or B).

3. *Arms:* Cut a lolly (popsicle) stick in half and cover each piece with flesh-coloured felt. (Fig. 2).

4. *Head:* Using flesh-coloured stockinette or a piece of very light-coloured old tights or stretchy stockinette undies matching the colour of the felt "hands" as nearly as possible, make a ball about 1¾ inches (5 cm) in diameter. (See page 8 No. 1).

5. *Hair:* Sew a tiny bundle of fine yellow or brown wool or stranded cotton to top of head, using flesh-coloured thread for a centre parting. Arrange hair neatly and stick to sides of head (look at picture). Draw red mouth and nose, black eyes.

6. *Assembling:* Stick and stitch head to body, tilting forwards so that Mary is looking downwards. Sew arms to sides meeting at centre front. Stitch "hands" together at tips.

7. *Sleeves:* Stick or stitch sleeves over arms like a patch, A's meeting at centre front and attaching B's at shoulder level. The front edge A—B should be loose and "flowing" a little.

8. *Fold of Robe:* Take a large dart as shown in picture at O, stitching in place. Stick or stitch piece to back of figure, noting the position of Y's and X on picture.

9. *Veil:* Arrange the veil on Mary's head, noting on picture that V comes at centre front, T at centre back and W on each side. Fold it so that it forms a large inverted box pleat at centre back, and stick and stitch in place as necessary to give the right effect.

10. *Halo:* Using pattern for Angel No. 1, page 95, cut a circle of gold or silver cardboard or use white cardboard covered with foil. Stick to back of head.

" . . . Mary kept all these things and pondered them in her heart . . ."
(St. Luke 2.19)

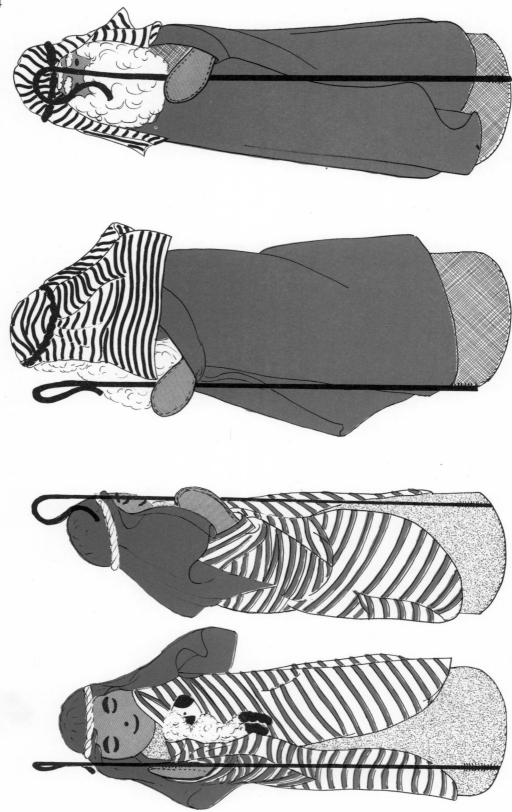

THE SHEPHERDS

"And there were in the same country shepherds abiding in the field, keeping watch over their flock by night . . ." (St. Luke 2.8)

HOW TO MAKE THE OLD SHEPHERD
(Read instructions on page 7).

1. *Body:* Cover a salt container with coarse, drab-coloured material. (Fig. 1 B).

2. *Head:* Using double thickness of top of tights, make a ball 1½ inches (2·5 cm—3 cm) diameter. Draw brown eyes. Stitch head to front edge of top of body, leaning very much forward. (See page 8 No. 1).

3. *Hair and Beard:* Stick a little cotton wool round edge of face for hair, a piece hanging downwards for beard and tiny scraps for brows and "moustache".

4. *Hand:* Cover wooden ice cream spoon with felt to match face and stitch to side of body. (The other hand appears to be hidden inside wrap). (Fig. 7).

5. *Cloak:* Cut a piece of material about 9½ inches (24 cm) square, round off the corners and arrange on the figure, stitching in place at one side.

6. *Head Shawl:* Cut a piece of gay striped material about 7 inches (18 cm.) square, and, folding the front edge under, place on head. Stitch and/or stick in place. Bind a piece of cord round the head and stitch in place.

7. *Crook:* Bend a length of wire to make a crook and stitch to hand also to base of figure.

HOW TO MAKE THE YOUNG SHEPHERD

Work exactly as given for the old shepherd with the following adjustments.

1. Shorten salt container to 7 inches (18 cm).

2. Omit hair and beard.

3. Alter face—look at picture.

4. Put hand on opposite side of body.

5. Use different coloured materials and plain for head shawl, striped for cloak.

6. For added interest make a lamb as given in the companion volume on the Old Testament and tuck into fold of cloak.

"And the shepherds returned, glorifying and praising God for all the things that they had heard and seen . . ." (St. Luke 2.20)

THE ORIENTAL KING

"Herod sent them to Bethlehem and
said 'Go search diligently for the
young child.'"   (St. Matthew 2.8)

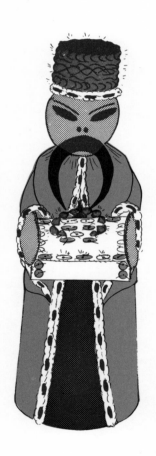

HOW TO MAKE HIM (Read instructions on page 7).

Use bright felt of a different shade from the other two kings.

1. Cut out eyes, moustache, sleeves and train (patterns pages 88, 89 and 90). Six pieces.

2. *Body:* Shorten a salt container to $5\frac{1}{4}$ inches (13 cm) and cover it with bright felt (Fig. 1). Stick a contrasting V to centre front and two pipe cleaners down each edge for fur.

3. *Hands:* Cover two wooden ice cream spoons with yellow felt (Fig. 7, page 25) and stick or stitch one to each side of body.

4. *Head:* Make a ball about $1\frac{1}{4}$ inches (4 cm) diameter (see page 40, No. 8 and Fig. 15) using yellow material (part of an old T-shirt would be ideal). Stick on eyes and moustache. Draw black brows and red nostrils. Stitch to front edge of top of body at a forward angle.

5. *Pigtail:* Plait together several strands of black wool to make a thin pigtail about $4\frac{1}{2}$ inches (11·5 cm) long. Stitch ends to stop it unravelling and sew to top of head. Catch in place at centre back so that it covers gathers on head.

6. *Crown:* Stick a piece of wide silver braid round head, overlapping at centre back and stiffening with cardboard if necessary. Stick a pipe cleaner round edge for fur. Cut a circle of bright-coloured felt large enough to cover top of head (as he has no hair). Push into crown and stick to top of head.

7. *Sleeves and Train:* Oversew pieces of pipe cleaner to these as shown on patterns. Arrange sleeves over arms (look at picture) and stick in place. Stitch train in place—arrange in folds. The stiff pipe cleaner edge will hold these in place.

8. *His Gift:* Cover a matchbox with bright "gold" felt (Fig. 5) to make a casket to hold the myrrh. Decorate with sequins and/or beads and if possible make a "handle" on top of the casket with a diamanté button or buckle or a strip of trimming. Stick firmly between "hands".

9. *Finishing Off:* Mark "ermine tails" using a black felt-tip pen, and decorate his robes with sequins, beads or gold and silver braid if you wish.

" . . . being warned of God in a dream that they should not return to Herod they departed into their own country another way."
(St. Matthew 2.12)

THE COLOURED KING

"The Star that they saw in the east went before them till it came and stood over where the young child was . . ." (St. Matthew 2.9)

HOW TO MAKE HIM (Read the instructions on page 7).

Use bright-coloured felts of a different shade from the other kings.

1. Cut out sleeves (pattern page 89). Two pieces.

2. *Body:* Cover a salt drum with bright felt (Fig. 1 A or B) and stick a contrasting coloured V shape to centre front. Stick four or five pipe cleaners to each side of V, making a wide band of fur, right up to top of body. Make similar fur round base of "cloak", i.e. on main colour only.

3. *Head:* Using brown stockinette or the top of a very dark pair of old tights, make a ball about 1½ inches (4 cm) diameter. (See page 8 No. 1.)

4. *Hair and Beard:* Using plenty of adhesive, stick black bobbles cut from bobble fringing closely all over head and round "chin", giving the effect of black curly hair and beard. Draw red mouth and nose, black eyes and brows. Stick and stitch head firmly to front of top of body, covering ends of pipe cleaner "fur".

5. *Arms:* Cover two lolly (popsicle) sticks with brown felt (or a shade to match head). (Fig. 2). Crack in the centre for elbows and stick and stitch one to each side of body.

6. *Sleeves:* Oversew two pipe cleaners round curved edge as indicated on pattern. Stick sleeves

to robe, almost meeting at centre back and pulling out fur-trimmed edge to give a loose effect. (Look at picture).

7. *Crown:* Stick a piece of wide "glittery" gold braid round head.

8. *His "Gift":* Cover a jar lid with silver foil for a platter and pile "gold" such as brass chain, blazer buttons and sequins into it, pressing them firmly into a thick bed of Copydex or Glue-all. Stick platter firmly to front of body and cracked left arm curved round the sides of lid. Rest the platter on top of the cracked right "arm" and stick firmly to this also.

9. *Finishing Off:* Mark "ermine tails" on the pipe cleaner fur using a black felt-tip pen and add any "jewels" and decorations you wish in the form of beads, sequins or gold and silver braid.

" . . . When they were come into the house, they saw the young child with Mary his mother and fell down and worshipped him . . ." (St. Matthew 2.11)

THE WHITE KING

"Where is he that is born King of
the Jews? For we have seen his star
in the east and are come to worship
him . . ."   (St. Matthew 2.2)

HOW TO MAKE HIM (Read the
instructions on page 7).

Use bright-coloured felt of a different
shade from the other kings.

1. Cut out sleeves, collar and crown
(patterns pages 88 and 96). Four
pieces.

2. *Body:* Cover a salt drum with
bright felt (Fig. 1 A or B) and
following the picture stick a
V-shaped piece of a lighter shade to
the centre front. Stick two pipe
cleaners down each side of this V for
fur and two round the base of the
drum on the main colour only.

3. *Head:* Make as given for Mary,
page 13 No. 4.

4. *Hair and Beard:* Sew a small
bundle of grey wool to lower part
of front of head for beard. Sew a
similar bundle to top of head,
hanging down the back for back
hair, and another bundle across the
top, hanging down each side. Leave
on one side.

5. *Arms and Sleeves:* Cover two lolly
(popsicle) sticks with flesh felt (Fig. 2).

Crack the sticks about halfway down for elbows (look at picture). Oversew a length of pipe cleaner round lower

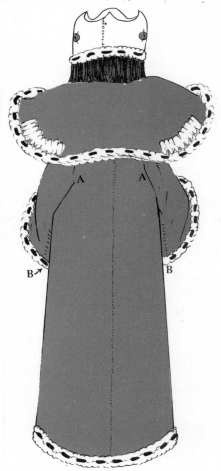

edge of sleeve as indicated on the pattern. Roll sleeve round, and, matching letters, oversew seam A—B. Oversew top short end A—C. Push an "arm" into each sleeve and stitch the top of each arm firmly to inside of sleeve. (The seam A—B will come on lower edge of arms.) Stick and stitch completed sleeves with arms to body. Catch "hands" together at centre front.

6. *Assembling:* Stick and stitch head to front of top of body, bending

forwards. Trim hair and beard, arrange carefully and stick hair to sides and back of head and beard to front of body. Draw black brows and eyes, red mouth and nose.

7. *Collar:* Oversew lengths of pipe cleaner to *both* sides of collar as indicated on pattern. Stick collar to back of robe, looking at picture, and when dry curl over top edge. The pipe cleaners will hold it in shape.

8. *Crown:* Oversew a piece of pipe cleaner round lower edge as indicated on pattern and decorate with beads or sequins. Overlap back edges so that the crown fits your king's head, and stick or stitch, forming a ring. Stick firmly to the top of head.

9. *His "Gift":* Cover a cotton reel (spool) with silver foil, pressing firmly and tightly in place, and with strong thread and a long needle thread one small and two large beads on to top of reel, pass needle through hole in reel and thread another large bead on to the base. Thread on another small bead then pass needle back through the large bead, the reel and the three upper beads, thus making a container for his gift of frankincense. Using the thread which holds the beads, stitch firmly to hands.

10. *Finishing Off:* Decorate the gift, collar and robe with sequins, beads and scraps of silver or gold braids if available, or leave plain if you prefer. With a black felt-tip pen mark "ermine tails" on fur.

" . . . and when they had opened their treasures they presented him with gifts of gold and frankincense and myrrh."   (St. Matthew 2.11)

The Baby and Manger

"(Mary) wrapped him in swaddling clothes and laid him in a manger, because there was no room for them in the inn." (St. Luke 2.7)

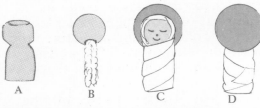

Fig. 3   Construction of the Baby.

HOW TO MAKE THE BABY

1. *Head:* Saw off the divided part of a dolly peg (Fig. 3 A) or stuff a doubled pipe cleaner into the hole of a wooden bead (Fig. 3 B).

2. *Body:* Bind all but the face to make swaddling clothes, sticking the end at the back (C and D).

3. *Face:* Draw features with red and black ballpoint pens.

4. *Halo:* Draw round a 2p (quarter) piece and cut out in silver or gold cardboard, or cover white cardboard with foil and stick to head smooth side forwards (C and D).

HOW TO MAKE THE MANGER

1. Collect twelve lolly (popsicle) sticks. If they are different lengths use the shortest for the ends and longest for the sides.

2. Make the end supports which are two crosses (Fig. 4 A). Glue them, then bind with strong thread for added support.

3. Join these two ends together with three sticks at each side of the manger (Fig. 4 B).

4. Add a lolly stick across top of each end (Fig. 4 C). Fill with hay or wood wool (fine wood shavings) and put the baby inside.

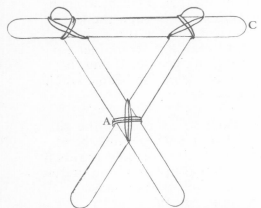

Fig. 4   Construction of the Manger.

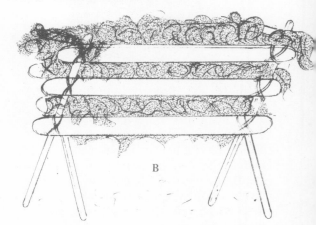

" . . . arise and take the young child and his mother and flee into Egypt and be thou there until I bring thee word; for Herod will seek the young child to destroy him." (St. Matthew 2.13)

The "dogs under the table" from matchboxes

" . . . Let the children first be filled:
for it is not meet to take the
children's bread and cast it unto the
dogs . . . yet the dogs under the
table eat of the children's crumbs . . ."
(St. Mark 7.27 and 28)

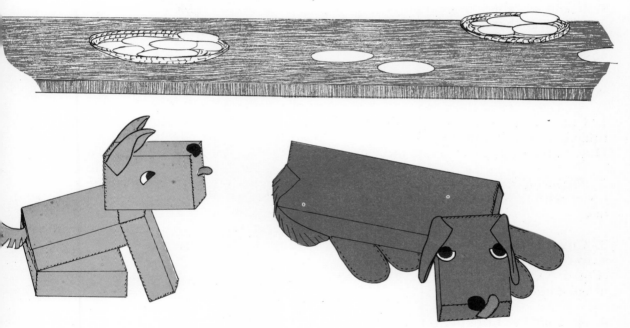

I wonder what these Palestinian dogs looked like—only the Gentiles kept highly bred species which were used for hunting. The "dogs under the table" were almost certainly mongrel puppies kept solely as children's pets, only to be turned loose or destroyed when they grew up. Adult dogs roamed at large, despised as scroungers and scavengers, apart perhaps from a few watchdogs.

Many of the "tables", at least in the better-off homes, were probably three-sided or a sort of horseshoe shape with "triclinia", so that often the family and their guests "reclined" or almost lay down on long couches to eat. In the poorer homes they would have been plain, rectangular wooden tables such as Jesus and Joseph made in their carpenter's shop.

I expect the puppies under the table were a little like wolves or hyenas, a real mixture, so I thought we'd invent two "matchbox dogs" of our own.

FOR THE SMALL SITTING UP DOG YOU WILL NEED

Four matchboxes for his body, legs and head.
Tissue paper for stuffing them.
Sufficient suitable "dog-coloured" felt to cover them.
Black, white and red felt for eyes, nose and tongue.

HOW TO MAKE HIM

1. Cut out the ears, eyes, pupils and tongue, also tail and nose for Large Dog, patterns page 91. Nine pieces.

2. *Preparing the Boxes:* Stuff the boxes with tissue paper to keep them firm.

3. Cover each one by oversewing a strip of felt round the main part (Fig. 5 A), then adding a piece to fit each end (B).

4. *Assembling:* Looking at the picture stick, then stitch two of the covered boxes together for body and front legs. A long, slim needle and ladder stitch, i.e. a stitch first on one box then on the other, is the easiest way to do this.

5. *Hind Legs:* Add a box for the hind legs, joining the lower edge of body and the top edge of the legs only, so that they are "hinged".

6. *Head:* Stick, then stitch head to body at a slight angle.

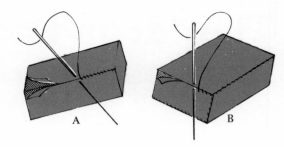

Fig. 5   Covering matchboxes.

Fig. 6   Folding dog's ear.

7. *Finishing Off:* Fold ears together at base and stick (Fig. 6). Stick one to each side of head. Add eyes, pupils, nose and tail. Finally add tongue, sticking carefully to front of head by the short edge only.

The Bible does not tell us anything about animals' tongues—but it does tell us about our own that " . . . the tongue can no man tame; it is an unruly evil full of deadly poison." (James 3.8). How true!

FOR THE LYING DOWN DOG YOU WILL NEED

Three matchboxes for body and head.
Tissue paper to stuff them.
Four wooden ice-cream spoons for legs.
Sufficient suitable "dog-coloured" felt to cover the boxes and spoons.
Red, black and white felt for eyes, nose and mouth.

HOW TO MAKE HIM

1. Cut out the ears, eyes, pupils, nose, tongue and tail (patt ns page 91). Nine pieces.

2. *Head:* Stuff and cover one match-box as given for the smaller dog, page 24, Nos. 2 and 3 (Fig. 5).

3. *Body:* Stuff the other two match-boxes, then join them with adhesive tape, making one long piece. Cover this in just the same way as the single box.

4. *Legs:* Cover the wooden ice-cream spoons by cutting two pieces of felt to shape and oversewing or stab stitching them together with the spoon between them (Fig. 7).

Fig. 7   Covering an ice-cream spoon.

5. *Assembling:* Looking at picture, stick then stitch the legs to base of body, working in ladder stitch—one stitch on edge of spoon and one on box. This is quite easy when a long slim needle that will slide sideways through the felt is used.

6. *Head:* Stitch the head to front corner of body and edge of one of the front legs—make sure you get the position "just right".

7. *Finishing Off:* Stick on tail, ears, eyes, pupils, nose and tongue.

" . . . There was a certain rich man, which was clothed in purple and fine linen and fared sumptuously every day. And there was a certain beggar named Lazarus which was laid at his gate full of sores and desiring to be fed with the crumbs from the rich man's table: moreover the dogs came and licked his sores. . ."

(St. Luke 16.19–21)

—so even the much-despised dogs were kinder than the rich man!

Two Woolly Sparrows sold for a farthing

"Are not two sparrows sold for a farthing . . ."   (St. Matthew 10.20)

These words are of course meant to indicate the commonest and most plentiful of birds being sold for the smallest coin in circulation—but go on to show the importance of each tiny creature in the scheme of things. Sparrows may be common but I love to hear them chattering round my home—I should miss them dreadfully and like all other birds they are very important to my family and me.

You could make a "sort" of sparrow in the same way as the mother bird on page 52, using light brown wool instead of black, but I thought you might like to create a more realistic bird in this case.

YOU WILL NEED

Oddments (remnants) of light brown speckled wool for body and fawn wool for breast.
Tissue paper for the foundation.
Fawn felt for wings, beak and tail.

A postcard (or index or file card) for stiffening tail.
Two shiny, dark-coloured beads for eyes.
Two brown pipe cleaners for legs.

HOW TO MAKE THEM

1. Cut out the wings, tails, and beaks (patterns page 91). Sixteen pieces.

2. Start with one bird.

Body: Make a ball about the size of a walnut for the head and one about twice as large for the body, using tissue paper and brown speckled wool and working as given for the hen on page 74, No. 2, Fig. 61 A, B and C.

3. Stitch the two firmly together (Fig. 8 A).

4. Wind a narrow strip of tissue paper round the neck to "thicken" it (Fig. 8 B).

5. Wind matching wool round the neck, over the paper (Fig. 8 C).

Fig. 8 Construction of sparrow's body.

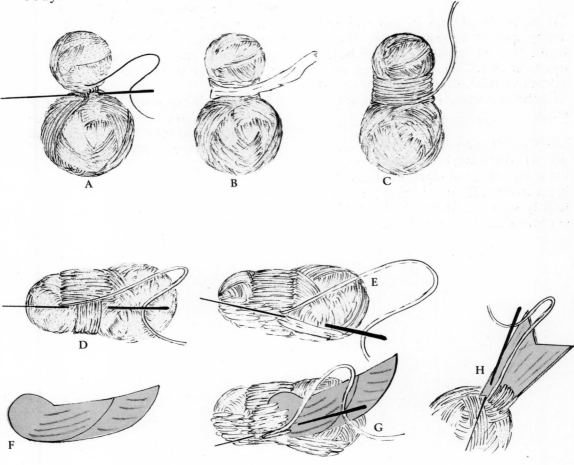

6. Take a few stitches with matching wool across from head to body, making the shape shown in Fig. 8 D.

7. Using light fawn wool take long stitches over breast (Fig. 8 E).

8. *Wings:* Stick wings together in pairs (remembering to reverse one) and with a brown felt tip pen draw feather markings (Fig. 8 F).

9. Stick one wing to each side of body, then continue with fawn woollen stitches, working over edge of wing to soften the outline (Fig. 8 G).

10. *Tail:* Stick the two felt pieces together with the cardboard stiffener between them. Draw markings. Attach tail to back of body with long stitches in the main colour,

which will also serve to soften the outline and join (Fig. 8 H).

11. *Beak:* Fold beak in half and with a tiny spot of adhesive across the inside of fold, secure it folded but open. Stick to front of head in an attractive position with a tiny smear of adhesive along outside of folded edge.

12. *Eyes:* Using strong thread, sew on two shiny dark-coloured beads for eyes, working right through the head from side to side and pulling tightly so as to form "dents" and slightly sink eyes into head.

13. *Legs:* Make legs as for mother bird, page 55 No. 13, Fig. 36 A, B and C, but make the "claws" a little smaller and cut $\frac{1}{2}$ inch (1·25 cm) off the top of legs. Sew them to your sparrow's "tummy" and bend and adjust them so that he stands firmly.

14. Make the second sparrow in the same way but try to vary the position of the beak and legs so as to give him a different appearance.

" . . . the very hairs of your head are all numbered. Fear ye not therefore, ye are of more value than many sparrows . . ."

(St. Matthew 10.30, 31)

A FISH PINCUSHION

"All flesh is not the same flesh: but there is one kind of flesh of men, another flesh of beasts, another of fishes . . ." (1 Corinthians 15.39)

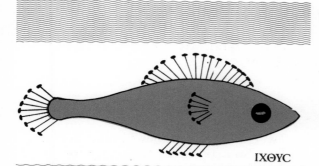

IXΘYC

Fish were much in demand for food and as we know at least five of the "chosen twelve" were fishermen. On Lake Galilee rods and lines, spears and several types of net were used. The fish were sold not only fresh but salted and packed in barrels so that they could be exported. Another great treat was pickled roes, expensive luxuries, reserved for special occasions!

The fish of course was the secret sign used by the early Christians. This was because the initial letters of the Greek words "Jesus Christ, Son (of) God, Saviour" spell the Greek word for fish, IXΘYC.

The little fish shown above is a quickly and simply made pincushion—his body is the cushion and the pins form his fins—there was one like this in my grandmother's work-box.

YOU WILL NEED

A small piece of gay-coloured cotton material for the body.
Bran or sawdust for stuffiing.
Two dark buttons for eyes.
Pins for the fins.

N.B. Bran is obtainable from any corn merchant, and is very cheap. It is advisable to use this for filling as it prevents the pins from rusting and polishes them nicely. Or you can use sawdust.

HOW TO MAKE HIM

1. Cut out the body (pattern page 92). Two pieces.

2. Place the pieces together, wrong sides outside, and machine all round on the broken line, leaving the opening as shown.

3. Turn right way out, stuff tightly and neatly sew up opening.

4. Stitch the two buttons in place for eyes, working right through head from side to side and pulling tightly to sink the eyes a little and shape the fish. Use white thread for this to make a highlight.

5. Arrange the pins at top, bottom, sides and end of tail for fins.

" . . . there is a lad here which hath five barley loaves and two small fishes, but what are they among so many?" (St. John 6.9)

The Twelve Apostles— a game to help you remember their names

" . . . He called unto him his disciples: and of them he chose twelve whom he also named apostles. SIMON whom he also named PETER and ANDREW his brother, JAMES and JOHN, PHILIP and BARTHOLOMEW, MATTHEW and THOMAS, JAMES the son of Alphaeus and SIMON called Zelotes, and JUDAS the brother of James and JUDAS ISCARIOT which also was the traitor."

(St. Luke 6.13–16)

You probably find these characters rather confusing particularly as there are two Simons, two James, and two Judases, several sets of brothers, several with more than one name and a great many fishermen! The words "disciple" and "apostle" are sometimes confused as well, so try to remember that a disciple is a "follower" or pupil of which all great teachers had many. An apostle is a kind of messenger and from his disciples Jesus chose the twelve men named above to send out as his first special messengers or envoys.

To help us sort them out I have thought up a simple game to play with the little "Smartie tube figures" shown on the opposite page, although I think that by just making them you will begin to understand

who is who. Most of the work can be either stuck or sewn.

FOR THE BASIC FIGURES YOU WILL NEED

Twelve Smartie tubes for the bodies. Two Smartie tubes to cut up for their heads. (Similar tubes may be made by rolling thin cardboard round your finger and sticking together as a cylinder). Twelve lolly (popsicle) sticks for labels. Oddments of felt in browns, fawns, greys for robes. Flesh felt for heads and hands. Odd lengths of brown, black, grey, white wool for hair. String or wool for girdles.

HOW TO MAKE THE BASIC FIGURES

1. Cut out the hands (eight double and eight single) (pattern page 92). Sixteen pieces.

2. *Robes:* Cover the tubes with various shades of drab felt by sticking a strip round each one (Fig. 9), then a circle to each end. Or if you prefer sewing, oversew the felt in place as shown for the Nativity figures, Fig. 1 A. Whichever way you do it, the figures need to be well made, secure and

SIMON PETER

ANDREW

JAMES

JOHN

PHILIP

BARTHOLOMEW

MATTHEW

THOMAS

JAMES THE LESS

SIMON

GALILEE

CANA

JUDAS

JUDAS ISCARIOT

strong as they will have to stand up to a lot of handling when you start playing with them. (I will explain later why drab colours are better than bright ones.)

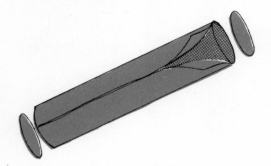

Fig. 9   Covering a tube by sticking.

Fig. 10   Making Apostles' beards.

3. *Girdles:* Tie a length of string or wool round waist, letting the long ends hang down at one side, tie a knot at each end (the join on robe should be at centre back). Place on one side.

4. *Heads:* Cut spare tubes into $\frac{1}{2}$ inch (a little more than 1 cm) lengths and cover each one in the same way as the robes—a strip round the side, a circle at each end (Fig. 9). The rings will naturally not have solid ends but this doesn't matter—stuff them with crumpled tissue paper for firmness and you will find the felt circles stick quite easily to this and the rim of the tube. (Or of course you can oversew if you prefer). Place on one side.

5. *Beards:* Looking at picture, stick tiny bundles of wool to the top of each completed robe (Fig. 10).

6. *Assembling:* Stick a head to the top of each robe, covering the top ends of the beards (Fig. 11).

Fig. 11   Attaching Apostles' heads.

7. *Hair:* Stick little bundles of wool round the top of heads for hair. Trim the hair and beards into various different lengths and shapes, then stick smoothly in place to top of front and sides of tunic.

8. *Faces:* Using black and red ballpoint pens draw eyes, eyebrows and noses. I think you will find they

The Twelve Apostles and their attributes

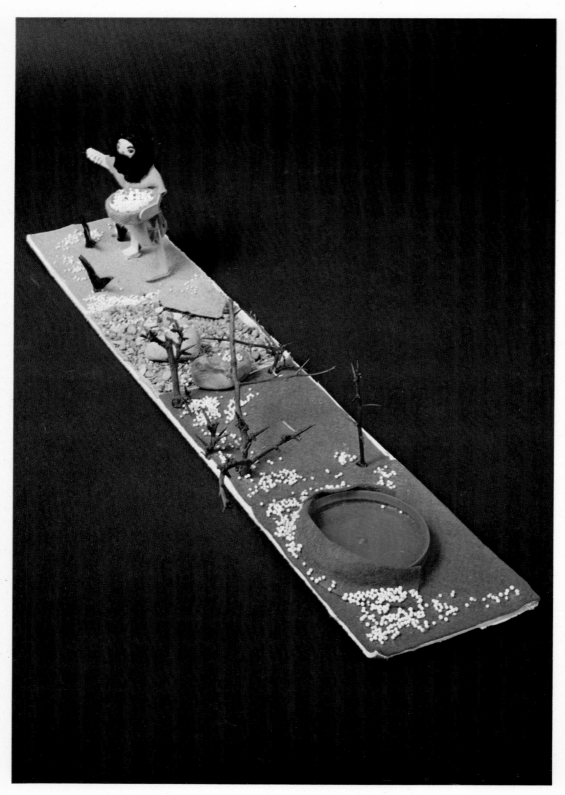

The parable of the Sower

look better without a mouth as this would be hidden under their flowing beards.

9. Looking at picture, write each of the twelve names on a lolly (popsicle) stick (Fig. 12). Place on one side.

Fig. 12   Back view of John with Mary.

These twelve basic figures now need to be sorted into separate personalities and characters. I have done this by attaching to them something to remind us of a story or incident concerning each one. Some apostles naturally pose more of a problem than others!

TO ADD THESE DETAILS YOU WILL NEED

Some tiny keys for PETER.
Two lolly (popsicle) sticks and a piece of wool for ANDREW.
A piece of net (sold containing sprouts, oranges, nuts, etc.) and a postcard or file card for JAMES.
A Smartie tube or similar small cardboard tube, some blue cotton material, a few crystal beads, scrap of flesh felt and a scrap of felt to match his robe for JOHN and MARY.
An oddment of "basket" coloured wool, a large button and scraps of "bread" coloured felt for PHILIP.
A twig and some green felt for BARTHOLOMEW.
Two blazer buttons, a drinking straw, gold or silver sequins and strong thread for MATTHEW.
A few large nails for THOMAS.
Two matches for JAMES THE LESS.
A piece of cardboard or index card for SIMON called ZELOTES.
Some greaseproof paper and the rest of MATTHEW's drinking straw for JUDAS THADDEUS.
A scrap of brown felt, some gold or silver sequins for JUDAS ISCARIOT.

HOW TO COMPLETE EACH APOSTLE

I think you will enjoy doing this— I did!

1. Cut out James' fish (as many as you like), John's sleeves (two pieces), Bartholomew's leaves (as many as you like) and Simon Zelotes' map (one piece). Patterns page 92.

Then start with

Simon Peter: " . . . thou art Peter and upon this rock I will build my church . . . I will give unto thee the keys of the kingdom of heaven."
(St. Matthew 16.18, 19)

Ask your family if they have any tiny keys, which they don't want any more. I found one from an old money box, one from a jewelry case and one from a brief case. Tie these into a bunch with strong thread, then make a loop at the top, slip Peter's hands through the loop and stick them firmly to the front of his robe. If you can't find any keys make some by bending wire.

Andrew (Peter's brother) : We all know the diagonal cross on the flag of Scotland whose Patron Saint is Andrew. Tradition tells us that whilst preaching in Greece this apostle was crucified on a cross of this type. Bind two lolly (popsicle) sticks together. Stitch to his "shoulder" at the back. Slip a thick piece of wool or string over his hands; stick the hands in place, then cross the wool and bring up over "shoulders", tying round the cross at the back—he will appear to be carrying his cross.

James, the Son of Zebedee, was one of the many fishermen among the apostles, so we will make him their representative. Arrange a small piece of "fish net" round his "shoulders" and stitch in place. Mark eyes, tails and fins on the cardboard fish. With a needle and thread make them into a "bundle". Tie the thread in a loop at the top. Slip James's hands through the loop and stick to the front of his robe at an angle. Stick the fish to robe here and there.

John (his brother) : "the disciple whom Jesus loved . . ." (St. John 13.23) was chosen by Jesus to look after Mary, His mother, after His death. (" . . . woman, behold thy son . . . behold thy mother! And from that hour that disciple took her into his own home."

(St. John 19.26 ,27)

Whilst making Mary, follow the picture very carefully. Cut 1 inch

(2·5 cm) from the end of a Smartie tube and stick a circle of flesh felt to the solid end for face (although this hardly shows). Stick a strip of blue material round the other piece of the tube for her robe, cutting it a little too long at each end and turning and sticking the ends over to cover the edges of tube. Stick the "head" to the open end of "robe", leaning forward at an angle—making sure the join in blue material will come at *back* of figures. Lay another piece of blue material over her head for a veil, arrange and stick the folds in place. Stick the two figures together all down one side, placing Mary sideways with her face hidden (no features are necessary). Sew on a few tiny crystal beads or pearls for tears. Stick John's hands in place, then cover the ends with his "sleeves"— the small one in front and the large one right across the back of both figures for extra strength (Fig. 12).

Philip was asked "Whence shall we buy bread that these may eat?" and answered "Two hundred pennyworth of bread is not sufficient for them that every one may take a little . . ." (St. John 6.5 and 7) when Jesus was faced with feeding the five thousand. To remind us of his connection with this story I have given him a typical flat, dish-shaped basket of the times, containing unleavened loaves.

Find a large button or cut a circle of cardboard about $1\frac{1}{4}$ inches (3 cm) in diameter. Using "basket-coloured" wool and working in garter stitch (plain knitting) knit a little square large enough to cover the button. I used size 12 needles (U.S.1), cast on twelve stitches and worked twelve rows. When you have cast off leave a long end, thread this into a needle and run gathers all round the outside of square. Place the button in the centre, pull up gathers and fasten off. Cut three or four "loaves" from suitable coloured felt (about the size of $\frac{1}{2}$p (dime) piece) and stick to top of basket having the gathered side underneath. Stitch basket to front of Philip's robe—you will find this quite easy if you use a long needle and take alternate stitches on robe and basket, working right round towards the sides of robe and pulling stitches tightly. Stick a hand to each side.

Bartholomew was a close friend of Philip. This was really his surname, his first name being Nathanael. I expect you know him better by that name. " . . . before that Philip called thee when thou wast under the fig tree I saw thee . . ." (St. John 1.48)

I have made a little tree for this apostle to remind us how Philip found him under his fig tree.

Find a spiky twig just tall enough to have "branches" above the head of your figure. (Mine came from a holly tree and was a very convenient shape after I'd trimmed off a few pieces.) Stitch this firmly to Nathanael's back, oversewing with a strong thread from top to bottom. Stick felt leaves here and there. Stick hands to front of robe, folding them at the centre so that they stand out and Nathanael Bartholomew appears to be praying.

Matthew was a publican or tax collector and no more popular with the majority of the people than tax collectors are today! He also had two names, his Jewish name being Levi, but it is as Matthew that he is best

known. "He saw a man named Matthew sitting at the receipt of custom and saith unto him 'Follow me' . . ." (St. Matthew 9.9)

Naturally Matthew would have used scales to weigh the gold and silver he collected, so I have made a tiny pair for this figure to hold.

Take a blazer button and tie a double length of strong thread to the shank. Cut $1\frac{1}{2}$ inches (4 cm) off a plastic drinking straw (yellow if possible). Do not throw the rest of the straw away. You will need it for Judas. Pass the threads through this and tie ends to shank of second button, leaving about 1 inch (2·5 cm) hanging at each end of straw. Bind a tiny piece of Sellotape (Scotch tape) round each end of straw to stop the ends splitting and put a spot of adhesive just inside each open end to keep the thread in place and the "scales" evenly balanced. Stick gold and/or silver sequins in place for coins. (Or punch circles of suitable coloured cardboard or paper if you have it—this is easier to stick and handle.) Tie a loop of thread round centre of straw, slip hands through the loop and stick to centre front of robe.

Thomas was a friend of Matthew—and was also called "Didymus" (a twin). Because he would not believe anything until he had actually proved it to be true he became known as "The Doubter". I expect you have often called someone "a doubting Thomas" when they don't believe what you say. After the crucifixion Thomas at first refused to believe that Christ had risen again and said: " . . . except I shall see in his hands the print of the nails . . . I will not believe." (St. John 20.25)

Tuck two or three large nails into the front of your figure's girdle, then stick hands over them, so that the apostle appears to be holding them. I think this is the best way to remind us of the story of "Doubting Thomas".

James, the son of Alphaeus, is usually known as "James the Less" to distinguish him from James the Son of Zebedee. The Bible tells us very little about him except that his mother was one of the women present at the crucifixion. "There were also women looking on afar off: among them was Mary Magdalene and Mary the mother of James the less . . ."

(St. Mark 15.40)

In order to connect him as far as possible with that story I have made this apostle a little cross to hold, and I think this will help you to separate him in your own mind from "fisherman James" the son of Zebedee. Cut two suitable size pieces of matchstick and fix together with adhesive to form a cross. When set, bind the join with matching thread, criss-crossing several times for added strength. Thread these cottons into a needle and sew cross to front of robe, again criss-crossing over the join. Stick the hands in place to give the appearance of holding the cross.

Simon Called Zelotes (or the Zealot) is another apostle of whom we read little in the New Testament. We know he was a Canaanite and quite a different character from Simon Peter, that rather "special" fisherman. To distinguish him I have made a little map for him to hold, hoping that this will help you to identify him. This is roughly the

shape of Galilee during the time of the apostles. Trace the shape (pattern page 92) on to a cardboard and mark in CANA. Stick the shape to the front of Simon's robe and stick a hand to each side.

Judas, the brother of James, may be better known to you as Thaddeus, or "Lebbaeus whose surname was Thaddeus" (St. Matthew 10.3). "He that hath my commandments and keepeth them . . . I will manifest myself to him. Judas saith unto him, not Iscariot, Lord, how is it that thou will manifest thyself to us and not unto the world? . . ."

(St. John 14.21, 22)

This rare mention of the "other", less well-known Judas gives us an opportunity to single him out by giving him a book of commandments to hold. In those days of course books were in the form of a scroll. Stick two thicknesses of greaseproof paper together to look like vellum or parchment and cut a strip about $1\frac{1}{2}$ inches (4 cm) × 3 inches (7·5 cm). Cut two pieces off a drinking straw, the remains of the one you used for Matthew's scales, each about $1\frac{3}{4}$ inches (4·5 cm) long. Stick one to each end of the strip of paper. Roll the paper up a little way at each end and stick in place.

Write "COMMANDMENTS" and a few "squiggles" on the book. Stick to front of Judas's robe and stick a hand to each side—holding it.

Judas Iscariot was quite different from the other apostles—I expect you know all about *him*. A money lover, he became Treasurer for the Twelve, known as the "keeper of the purse". " . . . Judas Iscariot, one of the

twelve, went unto the chief priests to betray him unto them . . . and (they) promised to give him money."
(St. Mark 14.10, 11)

Cut a circle of brown felt by drawing round a small sherry glass. Gather all the way round the edge with strong thread, pull up the gathers to make a little purse, stitch several times through the top, then make the gathering thread into a "handle" by stitching it across to the opposite side. Slip Judas Iscariot's hands through the "handle" and stick them in place in front of robe. Stick a few gold and/or silver sequins (or circles punched from appropriate coloured cardboard) to purse and robe to represent coins spilling out.

Finally push the correct name label into the back of each figure's girdle (Fig. 12).

Stand your apostles in a row, remove their labels and mix up the figures,

then see how quickly you can sort them all out and re-label them correctly.

You will probably understand by now why I suggested making them all rather alike and with drab indistinguishable clothes. I thought if you gave some bright coloured robes, made some clean shaven, gave some curly or short hair (as would really have been the case), you would perhaps be able to "cheat" a little and remember their names by their appearance rather than by their stories!

Regarding long hair, the Bible tells us that " . . . if a man have long hair it is a shame unto him" (1 Corinthians 11.14)—an interesting thought in this day and age!
" . . . and He called unto Him the twelve and began to send them forth two by two . . ." (St. Mark 6.7)

THE DEVIL

" . . . Your adversary the devil, as a roaring lion, walketh about seeking whom he may devour."

(1 Peter 5.8)

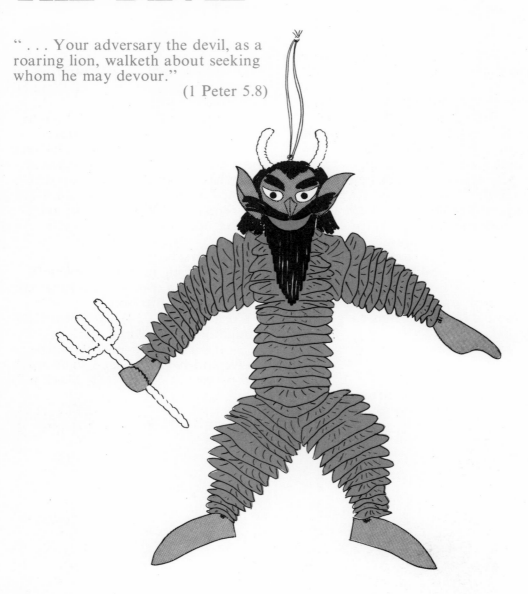

It seemed to me quite impossible to leave this character out of any book concerning the Bible, he appears over and over again in so many different guises and called by so many different names. Wicked angel, roaring lion, Beelzebub, Accuser, Deceiver, Belial, Liar, Lucifer, Satan, Tormentor, Wolf, Lightning, Locust, Serpent— call him what you will it seems best to portray him here in his red suit, complete with horns and flashing eyes and carrying his pitchfork!

Fig. 13   Preparing the circles.

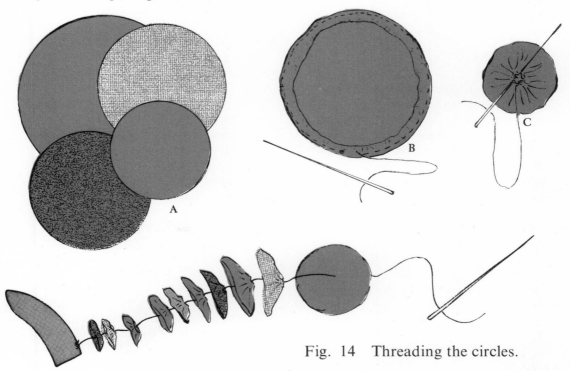

A

B

C

Fig. 14   Threading the circles.

YOU WILL NEED

A lot of odd scraps of red material. (Different shades of red are ideal but the material should be thin—cotton is best.)
Top of old tights for head and matching felt for hands.
Scrap of red felt for feet and mouth, white for eyes.
Two green sequins for pupils.
Grey wool for hair, beard and moustache.
Three pipe cleaners for horns and pitchfork.
Postcard for "base" of beard.
Strong thread for stringing up.
Small ball of cotton wool for stuffing head.

HOW TO MAKE HIM

1. Cut out the ears, eyes, nose, mouth, hands, feet and beard base (patterns page 96). Twelve pieces.

2. *Red Suit:* Drawing round the rim of a teacup for a pattern, cut out approximately forty red circles. Then cut out eight circles slightly smaller (a beaker?), eight smaller still (a coffee cup?), and twelve very small ones (a sherry glass?). The three smaller sizes will graduate and shape the limbs (Fig. 13 A).

3. Run a gathering thread round the outside edge of each circle taking a small turning (Fig. 13 B). Pull up

gathers and fasten off securely with a few stitches, thus making a flat "disc" (C).

4. *Assembling:* Fig. 14.

Legs: With a long needle and strong thread or fine string take a few stitches through the top of one foot, then thread on three of the smallest circles, two slightly larger, two larger still and about seven of the main size, all with gathered side uppermost. Place on one side.

5. Make another leg in the same way.

6. *Body:* Thread the two strings from the legs into ONE large needle and add about eleven more large circles. Place on one side.

7. *Arms:* Make these exactly as for the legs but use hands instead of feet and only six large circles. Thread all four strings into ONE large needle

and add about four more large circles. Place on one side.

8. *Head:* Cut a double circle, about the size of a tea-cup, from the top of a pair of old tights. Gather all round the edge, pull up and stuff firmly with cotton wool or kapok, making a large "knob". Fasten off the gathers at the back (Fig. 15 A and B).

9. *Ears:* Fold at base and stitch (Fig. 16). Stitch to head.

10. *Horns:* Fold a pipe cleaner in half by bending the ends to the centre (Fig. 17 A). Pinch tightly together (B). Sew to top of head (C).

11. *Eyes, Mouth, Nose:* Stick on eyes and mouth. Sew on sequin pupils. Sew two nose pieces together all round two long edges. With a cocktail stick stuff firmly, pushing the filling right into the point. Sew to

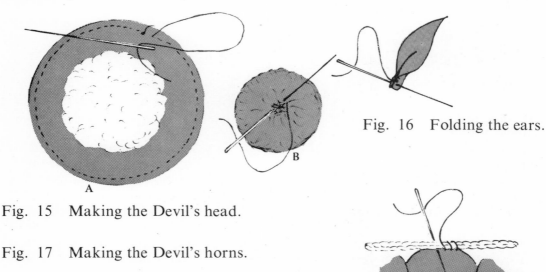

Fig. 16   Folding the ears.

Fig. 15   Making the Devil's head.

Fig. 17   Making the Devil's horns.

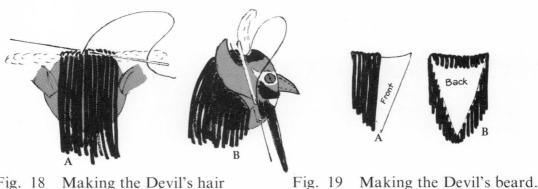

Fig. 18   Making the Devil's hair and moustache.

Fig. 19   Making the Devil's beard.

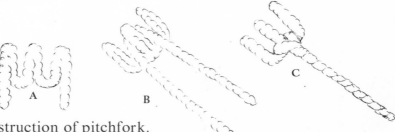

Fig. 20   Construction of pitchfork.

face curving downwards (Fig. 18 B), working all round—one stitch on face and one on nose alternately.

12. *Moustache, Hair, Beard:* Sew a tiny bundle of fine, grey darning wool between nose and mouth for moustache—trim ends. Sew a large bundle of similar wool to top of head for hair, so as to cover where the horns are attached (Fig. 18 A). Turn front hair over to the back, arrange it round the horns and stick "hair" neatly to back of head so as to cover the gathers. Leave the hair fairly long but trim ends. Curve horns upwards. Cover one side of card base for beard with Copydex or Glue-all, lay strands of wool over it, turning them over to the back on top, curved edge (Fig. 19 A and B). Stick to face. Embroider eyebrows and take a few stitches from sides of beard up in front of ears to join hair (Fig. B), and a few on face and head to make a "point". Look at picture.

13. *Pitchfork:* Fold the two pipe cleaners as Fig. 20 A, B and C. Pinch tightly and solidly together, bend to shape. Place on one side.

14. *Finishing Off:* Push the needle containing the four body strings (prepared in No. 7) right through head behind beard and bring it out on top, pulling with pliers if necessary. Arrange circles, each limb at a time, by pulling each string tightly so that the circles are closely packed and form a solid red body. Tie strings tightly together several times on top of head. Tie a knot a few inches higher to make a loop so that you can hang up your devil. Cut off ends. Fold the right hand round the handle of pitchfork and stitch in place.

" . . . that old serpent called the Devil and Satan, which deceiveth the whole world . . ."

(Revelation 12.9)

42

A COCK from plastic drinking straws

"I tell thee, Peter, the cock shall not
crow this day, before that thou shalt
thrice deny that thou knowest me . . ."
(St. Luke 22.34)

We all know the story of Peter and
the cock. I wonder if that
particular bird was brown or white
and whether he had beautiful
coloured feathers in his tail like those
we often see today. I made this one
from coloured, plastic, drinking
straws—he was very quick to do.

YOU WILL NEED

A box of plastic drinking straws in
mixed colours. (One box would make
three or four birds.)
Scraps of red felt for comb and
wattles; yellow for beaks; black for
eyes; white for wing backing.
A pipe cleaner to stiffen feet.
Strong white "button thread" for
tying.

HOW TO MAKE HIM

1. Cut out comb, wattles, eyes, beak
and wing bases. (Patterns page 93.)
Eight pieces.

2. *Tail:* Take nine or ten straws in
any gay colours and tie them together
in the centre very tightly, making a
bundle. Do not break off thread
(Fig. 21 A).

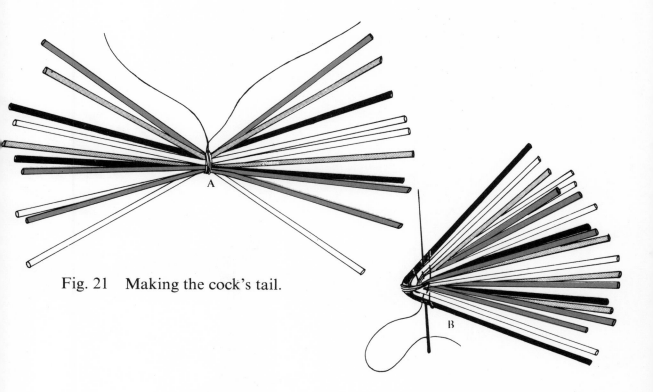

Fig. 21 Making the cock's tail.

3. Fold the bundle in half and using the attached threads and a long, slim needle, stitch backwards and forwards through the straws, close to the fold, to secure the tail in the shape of a fan (Fig. 21 B). Tie and cut off threads. Place on one side.

4. *Head and Neck:* Take four or five white straws and tie tightly together in the centre as in Fig. 21 A. Do not cut off threads. Put one of them at a time in a long, slim needle, fold bundle in half, then stitch together just under $\frac{1}{2}$ inch (1 cm) from the fold and bind several times tightly round and round (beak). (Fig. 22 A). Tie threads but do not cut off. Fold straws downwards about 1 inch (2·5 cm) further along and using the needle again pass the threads along to this fold and secure it with a few stitches (head). (Fig. 22 B). Pass the

threads about $\frac{1}{2}$ inch (1 cm) down "neck" and tie round and round very tightly (Fig. 22 C). Cut off threads. Tie the bundle again about 2 inches (5 cm) further down (base of neck).

5. *Legs:* Push two coloured straws up into the neck in the centre of the white bundle—these will eventually mingle with the tail (Fig. 22 C). Take three yellow straws and a needle and thread. Hold the head part and tail together and fold the three yellow straws over where they join. Stitch firmly, then tie yellow straws tightly together close to body (Fig. 23).

6. *Feet:* Cut two pipe cleaners into three (six pieces) and push a piece up into each yellow straw (claws) to stiffen them. Tie the yellow straws together about 2 inches (5 cm) away from body. Bend the six ends outwards, making a firm pair of feet.

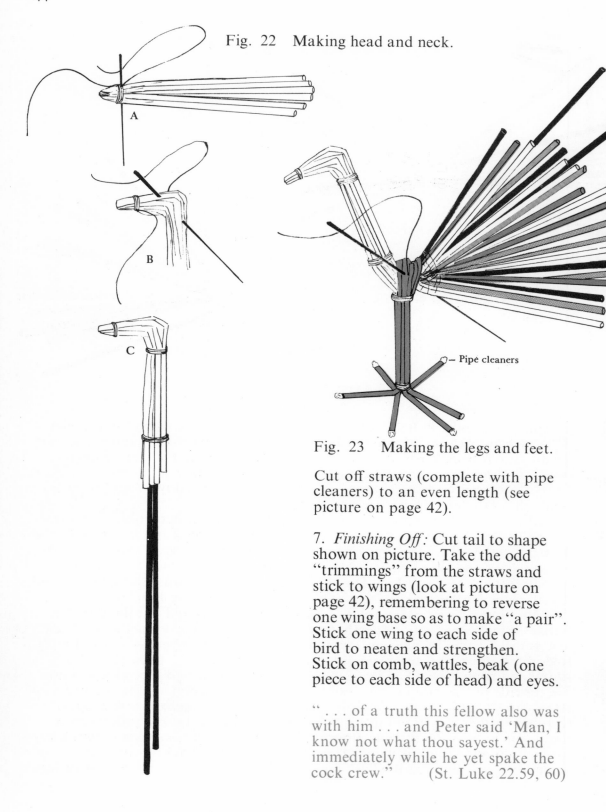

Fig. 22   Making head and neck.

Fig. 23   Making the legs and feet.

Cut off straws (complete with pipe cleaners) to an even length (see picture on page 42).

7. *Finishing Off:* Cut tail to shape shown on picture. Take the odd "trimmings" from the straws and stick to wings (look at picture on page 42), remembering to reverse one wing base so as to make "a pair". Stick one wing to each side of bird to neaten and strengthen. Stick on comb, wattles, beak (one piece to each side of head) and eyes.

" . . . of a truth this fellow also was with him . . . and Peter said 'Man, I know not what thou sayest.' And immediately while he yet spake the cock crew."   (St. Luke 22.59, 60)

A Paper Palm Tree

" . . . people . . . took branches of
palm trees and went forth to meet
him . . ."   (St. John 12.13)

Palms are of course among the most
prolific of the trees of the "Bible
lands". They are very quick and easy
to make from paper, and I thought
might be useful to you when
arranging the people and animals
from this book and that on the Old
Testament into groups or scenes.

Fig. 24   Rolling and cutting the
paper.

2. Paint the top third green on both
sides (the leaves).

3. Roll the paper up tightly and stick
the edge of the white part to the roll.

4. Paint the white part brown for the
trunk.

5. Cut all round the green part from
the top downwards.

6. If you have made a fat tree it will
probably stand up by itself, but if it
is tall and slim like mine, spread
adhesive to rolled base and stick to a
piece of cardboard.

The palm tree is a symbol of victory.

YOU WILL NEED

A piece of paper—almost any sort
will do, but the stiffer it is, the
stronger your tree will be. (I used a
page from an old ledger.)
Green and brown paint.

HOW TO MAKE IT

1. Cut a rectangle of paper as wide
as you want your tree to be tall.

" . . . a great multitude which no man
could number of all nations and
kindreds and people and tongues . . .
clothed in white robes and palms in
their hands."   (Revelations 7.9)

A WOLF in sheep's clothing — an "all change" toy

"Beware of false prophets which come to you in sheep's clothing but inwardly they are ravening wolves."
(St. Matthew 7.15)

This toy is rather fun—the mild, sleepy-looking sheep's fleece lifting off very easily to reveal a fearsome, ravenous wolf. The wolf only needs sticking, whilst the "sheep's clothing" is knitted.

FOR THE WOLF YOU WILL NEED

A Smartie tube (see page 6) for the body and a postcard for the head. Sufficient brown felt to cover them. Black and white felt for nose and eyes.
Four and a half brown pipe cleaners for legs and tail.
Tissue paper for stuffing.

HOW TO MAKE HIM

1. Cut out head, back of head, eyes, pupils, nose, tail, tops of legs and neck support (patterns page 94). Sixteen pieces.

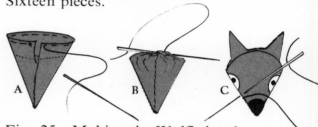

Fig. 25   Making the Wolf's head.

2. *Head:* Stick the cardboard stiffener to the felt head as shown on pattern. Roll round and stick in a cone shape (Fig. 25 A). Gather round top of "extra" felt, pull up and fasten off (Fig. 25 B). Stick the cardboard "back of head" piece between the two felt pieces. Stick this over gathers on cone piece, "ears" upwards (Fig. 25 C).

3. *Features:* Stick on nose, eyes and pupils. Take a few tiny white stitches on each side of "face" to represent teeth (Fig. 25 C).

4. *Tail:* Roll the felt piece round

half a pipe cleaner doubled and stitch (Fig. 26). Fringe edge.

Fig. 26   Folding the tail.

5. *Body:* Cover 3 inches (7 cm) of cardboard tube stuffed with tissue paper with brown felt as shown for the salt container in Fig. 1 B, gathering each end and pushing the tail into one end and securing in centre of gathers. (Look at picture.)

6. *Assembling:* Stick head to end of tube body—looking downwards. Stick "neck support" to cover join between back of head and body (Fig. 27).

Fig. 27   Position of neck support.

7. *Legs:* Twist the remaining four pipe cleaners together in pairs. Push pointed scissors straight through body at each end. Push the doubled cleaners through hole, bend downwards (Fig. 28 A). Bend them upwards back on themselves (Fig. 28 B) and twist (Fig. 28 C). Bend the "tips" forwards for feet (see picture), adjusting the wolf to stand firmly. Stick the tops of legs in place. (Look at picture).

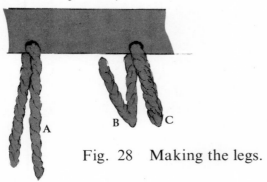

Fig. 28   Making the legs.

"Grievous wolves shall enter in among you, not sparing the flock."
(Acts 20.29)

FOR THE SHEEP'S CLOTHING YOU WILL NEED

Oddments of white and black wool in double knitting or two strands of three or four ply.
Size 12 knitting needles (USA 1).

HOW TO MAKE IT

Cast on 18 sts.
K. 1 row.
Work 1 row of "loops" as given for the bird's nest on page 53, No. 2.
K. 5 rows.
Repeat the last 6 rows seven times.

Head:
Break off white wool and join in black.
K. 3 rows.
Work in stocking stitch, knitting 2 stitches together at both ends of every K. row until twelve stitches remain. Break off wool and thread into a needle. Slip the needle through the twelve stitches, pull out knitting needle. Fasten off stitches by pulling up into a "bunch", and taking several stitches through backwards and forwards on the wrong side.

Finishing Off:
Run a gathering thread along cast on edge, pull up tightly and fasten off. Stitch a black loop into each side of fleece for ears.

You can now slip the sheep's clothing right over the wolf rather like a tea cosy!

"Behold, I send you forth as sheep in the midst of wolves: be ye therefore wise as serpents, and harmless as doves."
(St. Matthew 10.16)

Separating the sheep from the goats – a game for the very young

" . . . As a shepherd divideth his
sheep from the goats . . ."
(St. Matthew 25.32)

The shepherd's job was a very important and responsible one, every part of the animals he cared for being valuable in some way. Wool and hair for cloth, flesh for meat (sheeps' tails were a great luxury!) and milk to drink. Outcasts and "down-and-outs" dressed in skins when they could not afford other clothing. " . . . they wandered about in sheepskins and goatskins; being destitute, afflicted, tormented . . ."
(Hebrews 11.37)

The shepherd knew each animal individually and if one strayed would not rest until it was found. " . . . If a man have a hundred sheep and one of them be gone astray, doth he not leave the ninety and nine and goeth into the mountains and seeketh that which is gone astray? And if so be he find it . . . he rejoiceth more of that sheep than of the ninety and nine which went not astray . . ."
(St. Matthew 18.12, 13).

His flocks of sheep and goats were never allowed to mix—they were carefully separated so that he could drive the goats in front of him whilst he led the sheep.
I thought it would be fun to make some tiny sheep and goats, then turn them into a sort of game for the very youngest members of the family.

The miraculous draught of fishes — a "pocket" panel

"Foxes have holes" — a toy with movement

The story of the Good Samaritan — wall panel

YOU WILL NEED

A Polystyrene tile for the "board".
Sufficient green, very loosely woven
material to cover it—such as
towelling.
A few cocktail sticks or toothpicks
to support the animals and shepherd.
One or two white cards for the
animals' bodies, heads and the
shepherd.
Large size white bobble fringe for the
sheep.
White wool for the goats.
Pipe cleaners for legs and horns.
Black ink for marking detail.
Paints for colouring shepherd.
A piece of wire or pipe cleaner for
his crook.

HOW TO MAKE IT

1. Cut out the shepherd and as many
sheeps' heads and goats' bodies as
you wish (patterns page 92).

2. *The Pasture.* Cut the tile in half
and place one half on top of the
other, making a thick piece. Cover
this with loosely woven material.
Green towelling is ideal as it should
look like grass and have a sufficiently
open weave to allow the point of a
cocktail stick to penetrate easily.
The best way to secure the material
is to lace underneath with criss-cross
stitches of strong thread.

3. *The Sheep:* (Fig. 29). Cut a large
white bobble from a length of fringe
and squash and pull it into an
oval (A). Stick a tiny rectangle of
cardboard to the back to strengthen
it (B). Stick two short pieces of pipe
cleaner to the cardboard for legs (C).
Stick about 1¼ inches (3·5 cm) of a
cocktail stick to the centre of card—
point downwards (D.). When dry
stick a piece of adhesive tape right
across back to strengthen (E). Push
a cardboard "head" right into the
bobble at one end, securing with

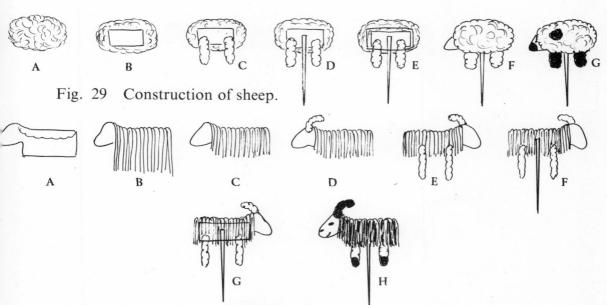

A   B   C   D   E   F   G

Fig. 29   Construction of sheep.

A   B   C   D   E   F

G   H

Fig. 30   Construction of goats.

adhesive; (ease the head and adhesive into place with the point of a cocktail stick) (F). Make as many sheep as you wish, then with black Indian ink, paint the nose, eye, ear and legs—on the right side only (G).

4. *The Goats:* (Fig. 30). Take a cardboard body and spread a little adhesive on both sides of top half of body (A). Lay a little bundle of fine white wool across the back and press down so that it sticks to the card at the top on both sides (B). Trim wool to shape (C). Stick a tiny piece of pipe cleaner to front of head for horns and curve it backwards (D). Stick two small pieces of pipe cleaner to back of body for legs (E). Stick about 1¼ inches (3·5 cm) of cocktail stick to centre of back, point downwards (F.). When dry stick a piece of adhesive tape across back to strengthen (G). Make as many goats as you wish, then with black ink, paint the feet, horns, eye, nose, mouth, and a few markings on the hair—all on the right side only (H).

5. *The Shepherd:* Paint his cloak brown or grey, his robe dull yellow, and his grassy hummock green. Mark in the folds and creases with black ink. Make a crook from wire or a piece of pipe cleaner and stick to back. Stick a piece of cocktail stick to back and finish off with adhesive just as you did the animals.

Now place the shepherd in the centre of the pasture by pushing the stick into the tile. Arrange the animals round him. As I think he must have dozed off for a few moments, let the youngest members of the family sort out his flock for him, so that they are ready to set out in search of fresh grass. " . . . and he shall set the sheep on his right hand but the goats on the left . . ." (St. Matthew 25.33)

Do you often look at a beautiful sunset and say "Red sky at night a shepherd's delight, red sky in the morning a shepherd's warning"? They were doing this in biblical times. "When it is evening, ye say it will be fair weather for the sky is red. And in the morning it will be foul weather today, for the sky is red and lowring." (St. Matthew 16.2; 3).

No doubt the shepherds were also among those who foretold the weather by winds and clouds. "When ye see a cloud rise out of the west . . . ye say there cometh a shower, and so it is, and when ye see the south wind blow ye say there will be heat, and it cometh to pass."
(St. Luke 12.54, 55).

A fatted calf and a swine from mending-wool cards

"Bring hither the fatted calf and kill it; and let us eat and be merry."
(St. Luke 15.23)

Mending was very much part of everyday life in Biblical times, just as it is today. We are reminded that "No man seweth a piece of new cloth in an old garment, else the new piece that filleth it up taketh away from the old and the rent is made worse." (St. Mark 2.21)—most mothers among us have probably made that very mistake more than once!

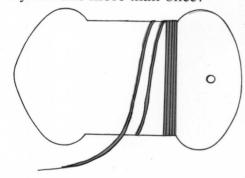

HOW TO MAKE THE CALF

YOU WILL NEED

Three pipe cleaners—three halves for each animal.
Paints or crayons.
An empty card for each animal.

HOW TO MAKE THE SWINE (or Pig)

Cut off one "bump" at the top and one at the bottom of the card. Draw the ear and mouth. Twist half a pipe cleaner through hole for tail and curl it. Fold the other two pieces in half and pinch together. Fold each one into a U and stick to back of card for legs. Paint the whole thing pink.

"He would fain have filled his belly with the husks that the swine did eat . . ."
(St. Luke 15.16)

Trim the "point" off the end of card and cut the main part narrower to make a long, thin neck. Make legs and tail as for swine, keeping tail straight and sticking legs to short, fat body. Cut a pair of horns from a postcard (pattern page 91 as for Ox) and stick to back of head—draw eyes and mouth. Paint legs, tail and horns brown.

"Thy father hath killed the fatted calf because he hath received (his son) safe and sound."
(St. Luke 15.27)

The birds of the air have nests — a "pop up" toy

" . . . the birds of the air have nests . . . "   (St. Matthew 8.20)

This well-known quotation is a wonderful excuse for making a nest full of baby birds to play with. As the cane is pushed and pulled the babies will pop up and down in the nest trying to snatch the worm their mother (who will also move up and down) has brought them.

YOU WILL NEED

A flat cottage cheese (or cole-slaw?) carton for the nest. About $\frac{1}{2}$ oz. of "speckled" brown/fawn wool for the "twigs"—(as used for the Sparrows on page 26).
A piece of cane or dowelling about $\frac{1}{2}$ inch thick × 14 inches (1·25 cm × 35 cm) long for handle.
Scraps of black felt for wings and tail and green for leaves.
Tissue paper and oddments of black wool for the birds.
Pipe cleaners for beaks, worm and mother bird's legs.

Bright coloured beads for eyes.
A scrap of black material about
11 inches × 3 inches (28 cm ×
7·5 cm) for the babies' bodies,
according to the size of your carton.

HOW TO MAKE IT

1. Cut out the babies' and mother's
wings, tail and leaves (patterns
page 93).

2. *Knitting the "twigs" to cover nest.*
Cast on twelve stitches, using size 8
needles (USA 5).
K. 1 row.
Now knit 1 row of loops like this:
A. Push point of right-hand needle
into stitch.
B. Wind wool over point of needle
and first finger of left hand, twice.
C. Then wind it over needle.
D. Draw loops through stitch,
leaving stitch on needle.
E. Place the three loops back on the
left-hand needle.
F. Knit the three loops and the
stitch together.

Repeat this all along the row,
making a row of large loops.
Work in pattern of 1 row K., 1 row
loops until the piece is long enough
to stretch tightly all round the cheese
carton. Cast off. Join short cast-off
and cast-on edges on the wrong
side, making the knitted fabric into a
ring.

3. *Nest:* Using a hot poker or the tip
of an iron, burn a hole in centre of
base of carton, just large enough for
the cane to pass through easily. (Or
cut a hole.)

4. Smear a little adhesive over sides
and a little way inside top of carton.

Slip the knitted "twig" cover on to
carton, turning the top edge down
inside and leaving about 1 inch
(2·5 cm) hanging loosely down at the
bottom. Press cover to carton to stick
in place (Fig. 31 A).

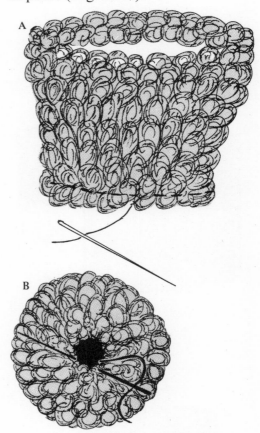

Fig. 31   Making the bird's nest.

5. Gather all round lower edge
(Fig. 31 A) and pull up to surround
hole in base. Fasten off (Fig. 31 B).

6. *Babies' Bodies:* These are made in
one mass. Measure the piece of
black material round the carton and
join the ends on the wrong side so
that you have a ring to fit top of
carton about 3 inches (5·5 cm) wide.
Put this piece on the carton inside
out and hanging downwards. Taking

a small turning, oversew the top edge to knitted nest cover all round top of carton (Fig. 32 A).

7. Turn the black piece upwards so that it is right side out. Turn in top edge and run a strong gathering thread all round. Do not pull up gathers or break off thread, but place on one side (Fig. 32 B).

8. *Babies' Heads:* (The original had six but you can add three or four more if you wish.) Make a series of balls about the size of a small walnut, using tissue paper and black wool and working as given for the Hen, page 74, No. 2, Fig. 61 A, B and C.

9. *Beaks and Eyes:* Fold $\frac{1}{3}$ pipe cleaner as in Fig. 33 A, B, C. Pinch tightly together. Paint yellow; allow to dry. Sew to heads. Sew a small, bright coloured bead to each side for eyes.

Fig. 33 Folding the beaks.

10. *Assembling:* Drill a hole about $\frac{3}{4}$ inch (2 cm) from one end of the cane. Take one head and stick to top of cane. With strong thread, stitch (for added strength) through hole and base of head (Fig. 34). Bind top of cane and stitches with adhesive tape.

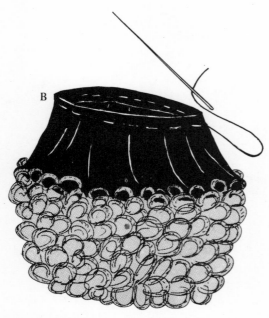

Fig. 32 Making the babies' bodies.

Fig. 34 Attaching the baby's head.

11. Push cane down into nest and out through hole in base. Pull up gathers on black material and stitch all round base of bird's "neck". (Fig. 35). Stitch the remaining heads here and there, on to the black body material—beaks all pointing upwards and in one direction.

Fig. 35   Assembling head and "body".

12. *Mother Bird:* Make two balls in the same way as the babies' heads—one the same size for her head and one about twice the size for her body. Stitch them together (Fig. 8 A). Add beak and eyes as for baby.

13. *Legs and Worm:* Paint two pipe cleaners brown for legs and $\frac{1}{3}$ cleaner red for worm. Fold legs as in Fig. 36 A, B, C and stitch to bird's "tummy".

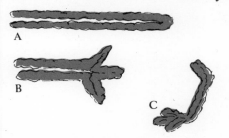

Fig. 36   Making the mother bird's legs.

14. *Mother's Wings and Tail:* Stick the wing pieces together in pairs to make them stiff and stick the cardboard tail between the two felt pieces. Stick end of tail only to body (from broken line on pattern), bend rest of tail downwards. Stick on wings.

15. *Finishing Off:* Stick a small wing upright to each side of each baby's head. Stitch mother bird to the side of nest to which the babies' heads are turned. Twist the red "worm" between the loop of the mother's and one of the baby's beaks. Stick a few green felt leaves to base of nest.

16. *Manipulating:* Push cane up and down. The babies will pop up out of the nest whilst the mother bird feeds them, hopping up and down on the side.

"Mustard is the . . . least of all seeds but when it is grown it is the greatest among herbs and becometh a tree so that the birds of the air come and lodge in the branches thereof . . ."
(St. Matthew 13.32)

N.B. Try planting some mustard seed in the garden and instead of cutting the young shoots to eat, leave it and see how tall it will grow. It should easily reach 4–5 feet and one of the directors of Sutton's Seeds Ltd. tells me he has often seen birds nesting in its branches!

Foxes have holes—
an animated felt picture

"Foxes have holes." (St. Luke 9.58)

These words and those on page 52 are used by Christ to give an idea of his own extreme poverty. He also likens Herod to this animal, well-known to us all for his craft and cunning, when he tells the Pharisees to "Go . . . tell that fox . . ."

(St. Luke 13.32)

The fox in this picture has a cream carton "hole" into which he is fastened by elastic. Every time you pull him out he will pop back again. Because foxes usually come out at night, I have made the sky dark.

YOU WILL NEED

A piece of very firm cardboard about the size of this page—for the foundation.
Navy blue felt for the night sky.
Two shades of dark green felt for fields and bushes.
Yellow felt for the moon, red for the flowers.
Brown and white felt and a postcard for the fox.
Tiny black beads for his eyes.
White thread for his whiskers.
A $\frac{1}{2}$-pint cream carton for his "hole".
A short piece of elastic.
Silver foil for the stars.

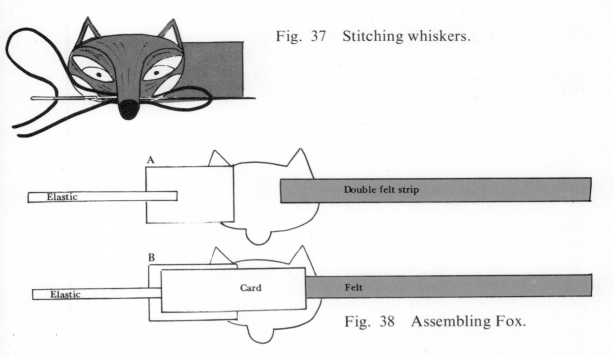

Fig. 37 Stitching whiskers.

Fig. 38 Assembling Fox.

N.B. You could substitute other suitable materials, or strong coloured paper, for much of the felt.

HOW TO MAKE HIM

1. Cut out the fox's head and body, the moon (five pieces) and a few flowers (patterns page 94).

2. *The Field:* Cover the board with dark green felt. (Remember it's night-time and the fields would look really dark). Turn the edges over to the back and stick them there.

3. *The Hole:* Cut the cream carton in half lengthwise and cover it with matching green felt, sticking all over and turning top edge over and sticking on inside of carton. Leave about ½ inch (1 cm) extra felt all down cut sides of carton (ready to stick to board later). Stick a semi-circle of felt to base to cover this.

4. *Sky:* Stick a strip of navy felt about 3 inches (7·5 cm) deep across top of board for sky.

5. *Fox:* Stick brown felt face to cardboard face. Copy features from pattern. Stick on white felt ear and cheek markings and eye patches and black felt nose, having first sewn the beads to eye markings. Make black shadings and marks with a fine felt tip or ballpoint pen. With a long needle and thick white thread take long stitches from side to side under nose (Fig. 37), leaving long loops at each side. Snip loops for whiskers.

6. *Assembling Fox:* Stick felt body to cardboard body. Stick head to body (Fig. 38 A). Stick the elastic (which should not be too stiff and strong) to back of body (Fig. 38 A). Cut a strip of green felt to match field about 8 inches (22 cm) long and 1 inch (2·5 cm) wide. Fold it in half *lengthwise* and stick, thus making a

long, double strip for extra strength. Stick this to back of fox's head (Fig. 38 A). Lastly stick a piece of postcard over back to make quite sure all the parts hold firmly together (Fig. 38 B).

7. *Finishing Off:* Look at picture. Try your cream carton "hole" in position and try the fox inside it so that he is only *just* inside and doesn't show (Broken line on picture.) Keep him in this position, while you remove carton. Turn the elastic round to back of card (B on picture) and stick firmly; cover the end (on the back) with a piece of postcard for added strength. Smear adhesive on the felt edges of the "hole". (You left ½ inch (1 cm) extra for this when you covered the carton.) Stick in place to cover fox. He is now hidden. Cut one or two bushes and large tufts of grass (no patterns are given for these as you can make them any shape), using two shades of dark green and stick them in place as shown on picture. When you stick the bush marked A on picture, slip the long felt strip attached to the fox under it and do NOT put any adhesive along this channel (marked by broken line on picture), thus leaving a slot through which you can pull the strip. Try doing this—the fox's head should pop in and out of his hole.

8. *The Flowers:* "Consider the lilies of the field how they grow; they toil not, neither do they spin: and yet I say unto you that even Solomon in all his glory was not arrayed like one of these . . ." (St. Matthew 6.28, 29).

It seems certain that the lilies of the field were not lilies as we know them but may have been the gay little scarlet anemones which grow everywhere, carpeting the mountains and pastures of those lands as the buttercups do in our own country. So add a few groups of red flowers and mark their centres and the grass with a black ballpoint pen.

9. *The Moon and Stars:* Stick a slim, new, crescent moon in the sky. "Let no man . . . judge you in respect of . . . the new moon" (Colossians 2.16) and add a few stars cut from silver foil. In this part of the world the stars are big and very beautiful—one feels almost able to reach up and touch them. Some seem much nearer than others, so make them different sizes.

"There is one glory of the sun and another glory of the moon and another glory of the stars: for one star differeth from another star in glory . . ."   (1 Corinthians 15.41)

The Good Samaritan — a panel for acting the story

"A certain man went down from Jerusalem to Jericho . . ."

(St. Luke 10.30)

This panel hangs up and has all the characters in the parable attached by long strings. Each one can be slotted in and out at various positions so that you can act out the "certain man's" adventures. Several of you can share in the making of this.

YOU WILL NEED

A strip of felt for the panel approx. 20 inches (50 cm) in a colour suitable for the "track".
Two knitting needles (or pieces of dowelling) and a curtain ring. Scraps of felt in dull shades of grey and green for the rocks and ass.
White felt for the roofs of Jerusalem and Jericho.
Flesh felt, and pieces of twig for the thieves.
Bright wool for the asses' reins.
Five small wooden balls with a hole drilled in one side (or big beads) for the heads.
Eight pipe cleaners, flesh pink wool and pink nail varnish for the bodies.
Black wool for hair and beards.
Bright scraps of material and wool for tunics and girdles.
Five halves of lolly (popsicle) stick and scraps of black felt for "attachments".

HOW TO MAKE

1. Cut out the ass, Jerusalem, Jericho, thieves' heads and arms (patterns page 96). Eight pieces.

2. *Basic Panel.* Roll the ends of the felt round a knitting needle and stitch in place. Finish ends with a neat sealing wax "knob". Sew on a ring for hanging up.

3. *Track and Ass:* Looking at picture, cut out and stick in place a series of rough overlapping felt "rocks" down each side leaving a zig-zag path from Jerusalem (stick this at top) to Jericho (stick this at bottom). Stick the ass in place, making sure he is coming from behind a green "moss covered" rock, so that he shows up well. Stitch bright wool round his head for bridle and leave a long, loose loop for reins. Mark his nostrils, eye and hairs with black ballpoint pen.

4. *Thieves:* Stick the heads and arms in place so that the men appear to be hiding behind the rocks. Stick on arms, "holding" a tiny piece of twig. Embroider hair with black wool and draw faces with black ballpoint pen.

The Travellers:
5. *Bodies:* Take a pipe cleaner, fold in half and twist ends back for feet (Fig. 39 A). Push doubled end into hole and stick in place inside ball (Fig. 39 B). Take half a pipe cleaner and twist across top of body for arms (Fig. 39 C). Bind the whole thing with flesh pink wool, covering each part twice by working down each limb, then up again. Start at

A certain man went down from Jerusalem to Jericho.

And fell among thieves which stripped him of his raiment and wounded him and departed leaving him half dead.

And by chance there came down a certain priest that way: And when he saw him he passed by on the other side.

And likewise a Levite when he was at the place, came and looked on him and passed by on the other side.

But a certain Samaritan as he journeyed came where he was: And when he saw him he had compassion on him and went to him and bound up his wounds pouring in oil and wine and set him on his own beast and brought him to an inn and took care of him.

(St. Luke, 10.30-34)

Fig. 39   Making "The Travellers".

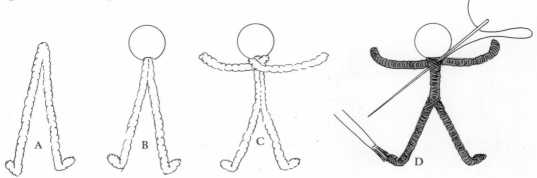

neck and finish off there by threading wool into a needle and stitching through several times to secure (Fig. 39 D). Paint the "tips", i.e. hands and feet, with colourless or pink nail varnish (or clear gum) to prevent the wool slipping off ends of cleaners. Stitch a twig into the hand of one figure for the thief.

6. *Tunic, Girdle, Hair and Beard:* Work exactly as given for the Sower, page 67 No. 3, Fig. 52, but of course on a smaller scale. Do not gird up loins.

7. *Face:* Draw with black ink.

8. *Attachment:* Stick half a lolly (popsicle) stick to the back of head, covering end with a strip of black felt (Fig. 40 A and B). This is to slot the picture into place in the panel. Make four of these figures—the chief thief, the priest, the Levite and the Samaritan, dressing them all in different colours and writing their identity on each stick.

9. *The Certain Man:* Make him in exactly the same way as the other figures but give him a little white loin cloth (Fig. 41) and make his tunic removable by giving it a front

only, with "strings" of wool to tie at the back of the neck (Fig. 42) then add a girdle. (You will remember the thieves "Stripped him of his raiment" (St. Luke 10.30)) and you must be able to do this too.

10. *Finishing Off:* Stitch a *long* piece of strong wool to the top of each head and attach to the top of panel so that the figures all hang down at the back. Read the story on page 60 and cut five small slits in appropriate places down the track so that you can bring the travellers forward and act out the "certain man's" adventures by slipping the lolly (popsicle) sticks into the slots.

11. *Acting the Story:* Start with the certain man in slot one, then when he meets the thieves and slot one is empty (the chief is in slot two), take off his tunic and leave him lying on the track "half dead" in slot three. Next remove the thief and replace him by the priest in slot two. He will "pass by on the other side"—so remove him and replace him by the Levite in slot two who will also "pass by on the other side".
Remove the Levite and do not replace. Put the Samaritan in slot four holding the reins of "his own

Fig. 40   Position of lolly stick attachment.

beast", and bring the certain man down, laying him on the ass's back in slot five ready to be taken to the inn.

———

I do hope this idea will help you to sort out the parable and that you will enjoy making the panel as much as I did.

———

"Which now of these three thinkest thou was neighbour unto him that fell among the thieves?"

(St. Luke 10.36)

Fig. 41   The "Certain Man" in his loin cloth.

Fig. 42   The "Certain Man's" backless tunic.

AN OX from matchboxes

" . . . thou shalt not muzzle the ox
that treadeth out the corn . . ."
(1 Timothy 5.18)

This curious old law of Moses is
repeated several times in the New
Testament — treading out the corn
referring of course to threshing. Oxen
were also used for ploughing just as
they are today in primitive countries.
To make this one

YOU WILL NEED

Five matchboxes.
Sufficient brown felt to cover them.
Tissue paper for stuffing them.
Scraps of black and white felt for eyes
and nose.
White postcard or index card for
horns.

HOW TO MAKE HIM

1. Cut out the ears, eyes, pupils,
horns, nose, hair and tail (patterns
page 91). Twelve pieces.

2. *Head and Legs:* Prepare three of
the boxes as given for the dog,
page 24 Nos. 2 and 3, Fig. 5 A and B.

3. *Body:* Make this from the other
two boxes as given for large dog,
page 25 No. 3.

4. *Assembling:* Looking at picture,
stick, then stitch the legs to body.

5. *Tail:* Fold the straight part in
half lengthwise and stab stitch or
oversew (Fig. 43). Fringe ends as
shown on pattern. Stitch to back.

6. *Head:* Fold ears as in Fig. 44.
Stick. Stick lower portion (below
broken line on pattern) to side of
head and fold and press ears to
"stick out" at right angles. Stick on
horns, eyes, pupils and nose. Fringe
hair. Stick the two pieces together
and stick solid part to back of head
over ends of horns, bringing fringed
part over top of head and sticking
there. Looking at picture, stick and
stitch head to body.

Needless to say oxen also found their
way into the cooking pot.

" . . . I have prepared my dinner:
my oxen and my fatlings are
killed . . ."   (St. Matthew 22.4)

Fig. 43   Making the tail.

Fig. 44   Folding the ears.

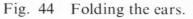

64

The Daughter of Herodias as a dancing paper doll

"... When a convenient day was come, that Herod on his birthday made a supper ... and when the daughter of the said Herodias came in and danced and pleased Herod and them that sat with him, the King said unto the damsel 'Ask of me whatsoever thou wilt and I will give it thee.'"   (St. Mark 6.21, 22)

No doubt you know this story and its unhappy ending when John the Baptist was beheaded. It certainly does nothing to endear us to King Herod! However poor Herodias' daughter was only doing as she was told and I like to picture her twirling and spinning to entertain her wicked uncle at his birthday party—whilst he probably reclined on a couch before the remains of the supper, occasionally eating the odd grape or fig, and lazily sipped a goblet of wine. This paper doll will twirl beautifully.

YOU WILL NEED

A piece of wire approx. 8 inches (20 cm) long.
White notepaper.
A drinking straw.
Paints or crayons.

HOW TO MAKE HER

1. *Cut Out* legs and body (patterns page 93) also a circle the size of a saucer in matching paper. Three pieces.

2. *Paint* (a) The leg piece pink with brown below broken line for sandals. (b) Hair black, face and arms pink, tunic any bright colour—on both sides of paper. Copy back from pattern and front from picture above. Draw black eyes and brows. Red mouth.
(c) Skirt on both sides to match tunic.

3. *Stand:* Bend the wire to form a very firm stand, filing the top to a sharp point (Fig. 45).

Fig. 45 "Stand" for the paper doll.

4. *Legs:* Roll the piece into a cone, overlapping so that A's and B's match. Stick firmly.

5. *Balance:* Take a circle of cardboard approx. ¾ inch (2 cm) diameter (the card disc at the end of a Smartie tube—see page 6). Punch a hole *exactly* in the centre (just large enough for a drinking straw to fit tightly into it). Smear Copydex or Glue-all round top of straw and push into hole (Fig. 46).

Fig. 46   Inserting straw into disc.

Smear the adhesive round edge of
disc and drop straw and disc into
cone, snipping a tiny piece off end of
cone if necessary—allow disc to rest
where it fits and snip off surplus
straw (Fig. 47). Place on one side.

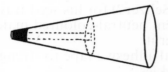

Fig. 47   Position of disc and straw
inside legs.

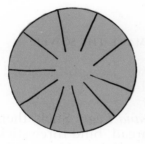

Fig. 48   Slashing skirt.

6. *Skirt:* Snip inwards as shown by
Fig. 48. Smear Copydex or Glue-all
round top edge of cone legs and
stick *exactly* to centre of skirt. Place
upside down to dry.

7. *Body:* Make three slashes as
shown on pattern. Bend first and
third tab forwards, second and fourth
tab backwards. Smear adhesive to
underside of each tab and stick
exactly to centre of top of skirt.

To make Herodias' daughter dance,
twist one corner of each skirt slash
gently upwards (like a propeller).
Slip the cone over the wire stand

and place her in a hot air stream
such as on a radiator, or a high-
powered light bulb. Adjust the foot
of the wire stand to grip firmly and
make sure a grown-up supervises
where you put her and says it is
quite safe. The heat will make her
twirl merrily round and round, skirts
flying. Any difficulty is probably
because your doll is not balanced
centrally or the hot air current is
insufficient.

"And she went forth and said unto
her mother what shall I ask? And she
said 'The head of John the Baptist.'"
(St. Mark 6.24)

Sower with seeds that really grow

" . . . a sower went forth to sow . . ."
(St. Matthew 13.3)

The little sower on the next page is quickly and easily made from lolly (popsicle) sticks. He stands firmly on any of the four types of ground on which he scatters his seed and when he comes to the good ground he plants mustard and cress which really grows! Several of you could combine to make this model, a different person being responsible for each of the fields and the sower.

YOU WILL NEED

A piece of very strong firm cardboard for the base.
Sandpaper for the "wayside".
Black felt and a postcard for the "fowls".
Tiny stones or "chippings" and two or three larger stones for the "stony places".
Rough, neutral coloured material for a base for the stones.
Brown felt or similar material to cover the thorny and good ground.
A small container such as a shallow, plastic jar lid in which to plant the cress.
A packet of mustard and/or cress.
An odd lolly (popsicle) stick to use during the making.
Seed pearl tapioca or something similar for "the seeds".
Three lolly (popsicle) sticks.
A wooden ball with a hole drilled in one side, or large bead for the sower's head.

Two pipe cleaners.
Black wool for his hair and beard.
A scrap of rough material for his tunic.
Wool or string for his girdle.
A small jar or bottle lid (Alka-Seltzer?) for his seed tray.
Sufficient neutral-coloured material to cover it.
Medical adhesive tape to strengthen his "ankles".
The family glue pot or some very strong adhesive.

HOW TO MAKE THE SOWER

"The Sower soweth the word." (St. Mark 4.14)

1. *Arms and Legs:* Stick, then using strong thread, bind three sticks together as in Fig. 49.

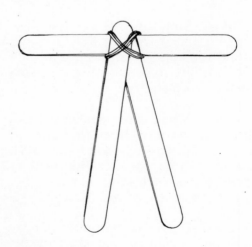

Fig. 49   Making the Sower's arms and legs.

2. *Head:* Take a wooden ball about 1 inch (2·5 cm) diameter—the sort sold in most handicraft shops that has a hole drilled in one side. Fold two pipe cleaners in half, spread the folded ends with glue and push ball well up into hole (Fig. 50). Twist and bind the ends of cleaners round lolly (popsicle) stick arms and legs (Fig. 51).

Fig. 50   Pushing pipe cleaners into head.

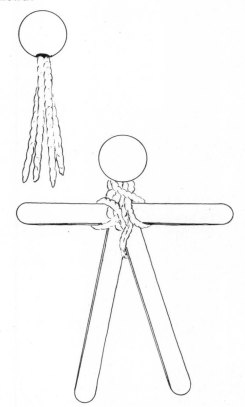

Fig. 51   Attaching head.

3. *Tunic:* Cut a small rectangle of "earthy" looking, rough material long enough to stretch from the sower's ankles up over his shoulders and down his back. Make a small slit in the centre (as small as practicable) and push head through

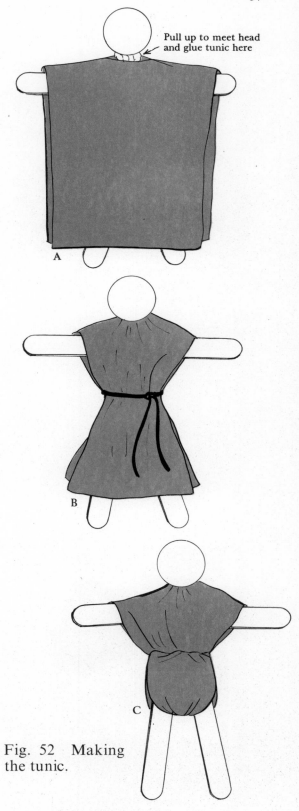

Pull up to meet head and glue tunic here

A

B

C

Fig. 52   Making the tunic.

this (Fig. 52 A). Glue tunic all round neck and pull in waist by tying a piece of string or wool round tunic for a girdle (Fig. 52 B).

All labourers used to "gird themselves" or "gird up their loins" before starting work so that their long skirts did not get in the way and hinder them. Thus the disciples were told "Let your loins be girded about and your lights burning . . ." (St. Luke 12.35).

In other words to be "ready". Gird up your sower by pulling the back of his tunic forward between his legs and tucking it into the front of his girdle (Fig. 52 C). I expect you see now where the word "girdle" comes from. (You can try this on yourself one day when you are wearing a long dressing gown!)

4. *Hair:* Stick little bundles of black wool to front of face for beard (Fig. 53 A) and down back of head (Fig. 53 B) and across the top for hair (Fig. 53 C). Arrange, trim, then stick ends to tunic to keep tidy.

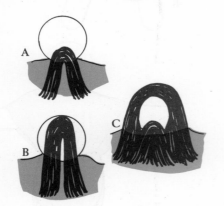

Fig. 53   Making beard and hair.

5. *Face:* Draw brows, eyes and nose with coloured ballpoint pens.

6. *Feet:* Crack the lolly (popsicle) sticks about ¾ inch (2 cm) from ends and bend forward for feet. Be careful not to break them off. Fix a tiny piece of medical, adhesive tape under foot and round "heel" extending a little way up back of leg, to strengthen and hold the crack (Fig. 54).

Adhesive
tape

Fig. 54   Cracking stick to make foot.

7. *Seed Tray:* Cover a small jar cap inside and out with a piece of neutral-coloured material by glueing firmly. Pour plenty of glue into the tray and fill it with tapioca or any small seeds, pressing them firmly in place and mixing the glue with the seeds. Stick a few seeds to the sower's right "hand".

Finishing Off: Crack the left arm twice to make bends at "wrist" and "elbow". Spread glue thickly all round one half of the edge of the tray and attach it to the sower's tunic and left arm, pressing it firmly in place.

HOW TO MAKE THE GROUND

1.   Cut out the birds (pattern page 92). Nine pieces.

2. *The Base:* Choose a firm, strong piece of cardboard that will not "whip", or stick two pieces together. Make sure that although it is strong you can push pins into it. Cut a strip about 20 inches × 4 inches (51 cm × 10 cm). Then roughly mark it into four sections, one for each type of ground.

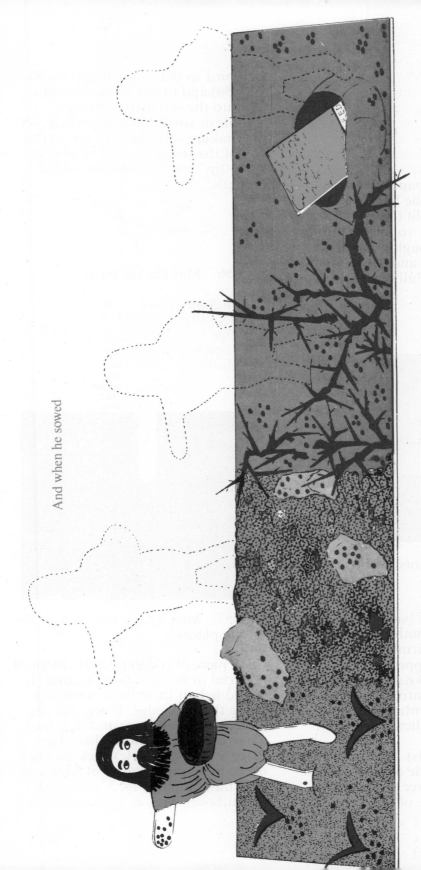

And when he sowed

Some seeds fell by the way side, and the fowls came and devoured them up.

Some fell upon stony places, where they had not much earth: And forthwith they sprung up, because they had no deepness of earth: And when the sun was up, they were scorched; And because they had no root they withered away.

And some fell among thorns; And the thorns sprung up and choked them.

But other fell into good ground, and brought forth fruit. . . .

St. Matthew 13:(4-8)

3. *The Wayside:* "When any one heareth the word of the kingdom and understandeth it not, then cometh the wicked one and catcheth away that which was sown in his heart. This is he which receiveth seed by the wayside." (St. Matthew 13.19) Cut a piece of sandpaper to cover the first quarter of the board. In the centre, cut a small slit (from end to end), large enough to push a lolly (popsicle) stick through quite easily. Turn the paper over and pencil round the stick (Fig. 55). Pull out stick.

Fig. 55 Making slots for the Sower's foot.

Spread glue all over back of paper *except* on the part outlined by shape of stick, and press firmly to board, at the same time slipping the stick back into slit to make sure that a free "channel" is left—into which the sower's feet will eventually fit. Remove the stick when glue is dry.

4. *The Fowls:* (Birds). Stick a black felt shape to each side of a card shape so that you have three strong birds. Slip a pin down one of the wings of each bird so that only the tip shows (Fig. 56) and firmly push these pin tips into the sandpaper, using a thimble or small hammer to help you and making sure they are not in the way of the sower. A spot of glue at each "tip" would make for added strength.

Fig. 56 Making the birds.

5. *The Stony Places:* "But he that receiveth the seed into stony places, the same is he that heareth the word and anon with joy receiveth it." (St. Matthew 13.20).

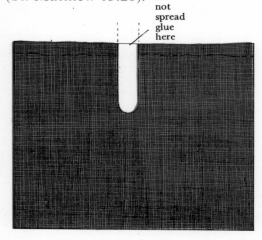

Fig. 57 Making the foot slot in the "stony places".

Cut a piece of rough neutral-coloured material to fit the second section. It would help if there were a selvedge along the *back* edge. If not, cut the piece a little too large and glue back a narrow turning along this edge. Place a lolly (popsicle) stick on back of the material at centre of back edge and draw round (Fig. 57). Spread glue all over back of material *except* this outlined portion, and press firmly to board pushing a stick into the "slot" to keep a free passage for sower's feet. (This time he has to stand at the back of the piece of ground because the centre will be too uneven.)

6. Leaving the stick in the slot, spread glue thickly all over this section and sprinkle tiny stones or chippings over it, pressing them firmly into place. Using plenty of strong glue, stick two or three larger stones here and there for boulders, making sure they are not in the way of the sower. Remove lolly (popsicle) stick.

7. *The Thorns:* "He also that receiveth seed among the thorns is he that heareth the word; and the care of this world and the deceitfulness of riches choke the word and he becometh unfruitful." (St. Matthew 13.22)

Stick a piece of brown felt over the last *two* sections of board, making a slit in and keeping a free slot for foot in the centre of this section (the thorns) only (see Fig. 55 and No. 3, the Wayside). Cut a pile of short prickly twigs (hawthorn, with the leaves stripped off in summertime, is ideal). Push drawing pins upwards from underside of board so that there are a series of little "spikes" showing through felt. Put a knob of glue on base of twigs, then push on to spikes, making sure you leave room for the sower to stand in the slot.

8. *The Good Ground:* "But he that receiveth seed into the good ground is he that heareth the word and understandeth it; which also beareth fruit and bringeth forth, some an hundredfold, some sixty, some thirty." (St. Matthew 13.23)

Find a small, shallow plastic jar lid (brown, if possible). (Maxwell House Coffee?) Glue the front half of it only to the brown felt on the board, as the sower's foot will tuck under the back of it this time, instead of into a slot. Glue some uneven strips of brown felt round the front of outside edge to disguise it.

9. *Scattering the Seeds:* When all the glue is quite dry and you are sure that everything is firmly set, paint clear gum here and there on all sections and scatter tapioca (or seeds) on it, pressing well down. Leave to set overnight, then tap off surplus.

10. *Finishing Off:* Put a little packet of mustard and/or cress in the container on the good ground ready to plant when you wish, using a few spoonfuls of soil and remembering to water it! " . . . the earth which drinketh in the rain that cometh oft upon it, and bringeth forth herbs meet for them by whom it is dressed." (Hebrews 6.7)

You can easily scrape out the container with a spoon and start again when you have eaten your cress! (See note at foot of page 55). Your sower can now be moved about and stand in any of the "fields", forever scattering his seed.

"Now he that ministereth seed to the sower both minister bread for your food, and multiply your seed sown . . ." (2 Corinthians 9.10)

A SCORPION from paper and pipe cleaners

" . . . I give you power to tread on serpents and scorpions."

(St. Luke 10.19)

We made a serpent in the companion volume on the Old Testament so I thought it would be a good idea to include instructions for a scorpion in this book. These dreaded creatures with their large claws and armed tail capable of inflicting a deadly sting, look rather like baby lobsters. As they love the dark and warmth they have a nasty habit of crawling into beds, pockets or shoes! In the quotation above they are of course signifying the devil.

YOU WILL NEED

Four pipe cleaners.
Some firm paper.

HOW TO MAKE HIM

1. Cut out large strip of paper (as shown at the foot of this page) for the body and nine small strips for the tail, claws and head.

2. *Body:* Take a pipe cleaner. Smear the large strip of paper with Copydex or Glue-all. Apply wide end to almost one end of cleaner and roll the paper round and round until all used up (Fig. 58).

3. *Tail:* Repeat this, sticking and rolling six of the smaller strips in place (Fig. 58).

Fig. 58 Rolling paper for the scorpion's body.

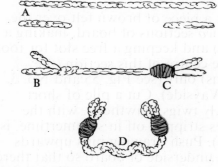

Fig. 59 Making the claws.

4. *Claws:* Cut one third off a pipe cleaner, then cut this small piece in two (Fig. 59 A). Twist one of these

pieces on to each end of the remaining two thirds of cleaner for claws (Fig. 59 B). Stick and roll one of the smaller strips of paper over joins, just as you made the tail sections (Fig. 59 C). Bend piece to shape shown (Fig. 59 D).

5. *Head:* Use the remaining strip of paper to make a roll as you did the other pieces, but this time there will be no pipe cleaner in the centre.

6. *Legs:* Cut the remaining two pipe cleaners in half.

7. *Assembling:* Stick the legs as far towards the head end of body as possible. Stick a strip of paper down centre for added strength. Trim legs so that each pair gets shorter towards the head; bend downwards a little, curve ends (Fig. 60). Place feelers at head end of body, stick firmly then bend protruding piece of pipe cleaner back over join for extra strength.

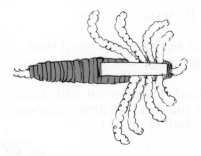

Fig. 60   Assembling scorpion.

Stick head over this join. Paint your scorpion black or, if you prefer, a bright imaginative colour.

" . . . they had tails like scorpions and there were stings in their tails."
(Revelation 9.10)

A HEN and her chicks

"... as a hen gathereth her chickens
under her wings ..."

(St. Matthew 23.37)

It is interesting to read of the example
of a hen being used during the
denunciation of the scribes and
Pharisees, and one wonders just when
these birds first appeared on the
domestic scene. Hens and their eggs
were quite unknown in Old
Testament times, although of course
the Israelites ate wild birds such as
quail and partridge, also their eggs.

Our hen is covered with simple
knitting, although there is no
mention of this craft in the Bible
and we presume it was unknown in
Palestine during this period.

YOU WILL NEED

A Primula cheese box for the hen's
body.
Tissue paper for stuffing.
Oddments of double knitting wool in
white or brown for the hen.
Oddments of fine yellow wool or
embroidery cotton for chickens.
Scraps of yellow, red and orange
felt for beaks.

Two white shirt buttons, two medium
size black beads and six tiny black
beads for eyes.
A pair of size 9 or 10 knitting
needles (USA 4 or 3).

HOW TO MAKE THE HEN

1. Cut out the comb and beak
(pattern page 94). Two pieces.

2. *Head:* Using wool and tissue
paper make a ball about the size of
a golf ball (Fig. 61).

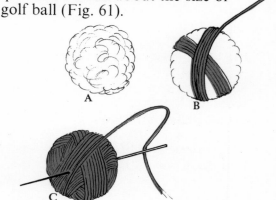

Fig. 61 Making the hen's head.

(A) Crumple the paper tightly into the required size.

(B) Wind the wool firmly over it until (C) the paper is completely covered. Thread the end into a long needle and take several stitches backwards and forwards through the ball, securing any strands of wool likely to slip. Cut off end.

3. Sew comb to top of head and a white button with a black bead on top of it to each side for eyes. Place on one side.

4. *Body:* Stuff the box with tissue paper to avoid crushing and seal with Sellotape (Scotch tape) to keep it closed.

5. Cast on 24 sts. K. 30 rows loosely in garter stitch (plain knitting). Cast off.

6. Fold the piece of knitting in half and sew up side seams to make a "bag".

7. Turn box upside down and pull and stretch the "bag" over it. Oversew the cast-on and cast-off edges together all along top of back. (If the colour on the box shows through, cover it with white paper first.)

8. *Wings:* Cast on 12 sts. K. 1 row. Work in garter stitch for twelve rows, increasing at the beginning of every other row, thus keeping one end straight and one shaped (look at picture). You now have 18 sts. K. 2 rows. Cast off.

9. Make another wing in the same way and sew one to each side of body; short, straight end to the front.

Leave long, top edge loose to make a "pocket". Sew on head.

HOW TO MAKE THE CHICKENS

1. Cut out beaks (pattern page 94)—one for each chick.

2. Using fine yellow wool or embroidery cotton and tissue paper make two little balls as shown for the hen's head (Fig. 61). Make one for the head as small as your fingers will allow—about the size of a marble—and one for the body just a little larger.

3. Sew the two together.

4. Fold the beak in half and sew to front of head.

5. Sew a tiny, black bead each side of head for eyes, or embroider with stranded cotton.

6. Make as many chickens as you like. (I made three.) Then tuck them "under her wings", i.e. into the pockets.

"... if (a son) shall ask for an egg, will (his father) give him a scorpion?"
(St. Luke 11.12)

A camel that will not go through the eye of a needle

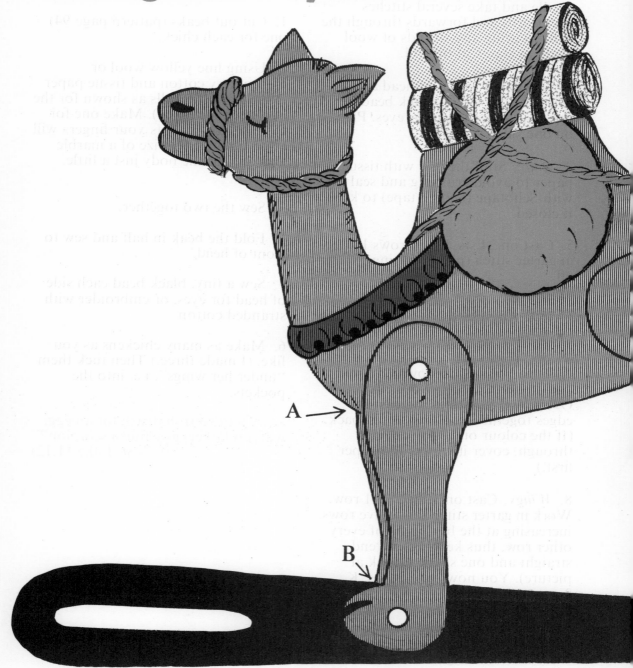

A

B

"It is easier for a camel to go through the eye of a needle than for a rich man to enter into the kingdom of God."   (St. Matthew 19.24)

This simple cardboard model, in which the camel takes up all sorts of peculiar positions as though struggling to get through the eye of a needle, can be decorated by painting or by sticking on felt, cords and braid.

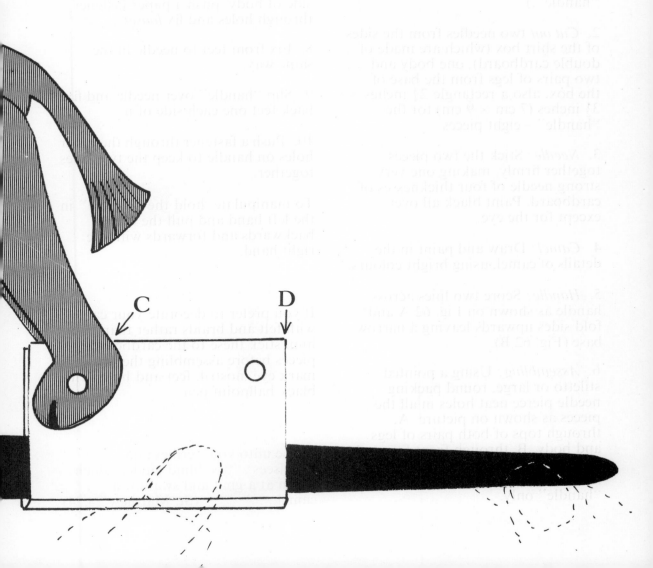

YOU WILL NEED

An empty shirt box.
Five brass paper fasteners.
Paints (or materials as mentioned above).

HOW TO MAKE IT.

1. *Trace* the needle, two legs and rest of the body (complete with pack) all separately, from the picture on pages 76 and 77. Four pieces. (Continue the outlines of body and needle where they are hidden behind the legs and "handle".)

2. *Cut out* two needles from the sides of the shirt box (which are made of double cardboard), one body and two pairs of legs from the base of the box, also a rectangle $2\frac{3}{4}$ inches × $3\frac{1}{2}$ inches (7 cm × 9 cm) for the "handle"—eight pieces.

3. *Needle:* Stick the two pieces together firmly, making one very strong needle of four thicknesses of cardboard. Paint black all over except for the eye.

4. *Camel:* Draw and paint in the details of camel, using bright colours.

5. *Handle:* Score two lines across handle as shown on Fig. 62 A and fold sides upwards leaving a narrow base (Fig. 62 B).

6. *Assembling:* Using a pointed stiletto or large, round packing needle pierce neat holes in all the pieces as shown on picture. A, through tops of both pairs of legs and body. B, through front feet and needle. C, through back feet and handle. D, through two sides of "handle" only.

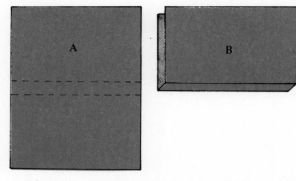

Fig. 62   Making a handle for the camel.

7. Place both pairs of legs one each side of body, push a paper fastener through holes and fix *loosely.*

8. Fix front feet to needle in the same way.

9. Slip "handle" over needle and fix back feet one each side of it.

10. Push a fastener through the other holes on handle to keep the two sides together.

To manipulate, hold the "handle" in the left hand and pull the needle backwards and forwards with the right hand.

If you prefer to decorate your camel with felt and braids rather than paint him, stick these to the cardboard pieces before assembling the toy and mark eye, nostril, feet and hairs with black ballpoint pen.

"Woe unto you, scribes and Pharisees . . . ye blind guides which strain at a gnat and swallow a camel . . ."   (St. Matthew 23.24)

The miraculous draft of fishes:— a pocket picture with a net that catches felt fish

"Master, we have toiled all the night and have taken nothing: nevertheless at thy word I will let down the net . . ." (St. Luke 5.5)

The fishermen in the picture shown on pages 80 and 81 can be lifted in and out of the boat. The net has a magnet stitched to it, so that when dipped into "the sea" it catches felt fish by pin heads at their nose and tail! As the men have been toiling "all night", I have made a large sun rising over navy blue hills, and the sky and sea of Galilee deep purple with a "sun path" across it. It looks like being a fine day, for the sky is not red (see page 50), but the hot sun will quickly dry up the flowers and grass. "For the sun is no sooner risen with a burning heat but it withereth the grass and the flower thereof falleth . . ." (James 1.1·1)

YOU WILL NEED

A piece of strong cardboard about the size of two pages of this book (see picture pages 82 and 83). Sufficient purple (or blue?) material to cover it and a little extra. Navy blue felt for hills. Orange felt for sun and "sun path". Black felt for the boat. Flesh felt for fishermen's bodies. Bright coloured scraps of felt for fish.

Black, grey, white and brown wool for hair and rigging. Thin white cardboard for sail, mast, boat foundation and fish stiffeners. Black ink to colour mast, etc. A piece of netting (vegetable bag?) Pipe cleaners and cotton wool to stuff fishermen. Scraps of gay material for their tunics. A very small magnet (toy shop or ironmonger). Steel pins to insert in fish. A shallow box for "trough" in sea.

HOW TO MAKE IT

1. Cut out the fishermen and fish (patterns page 95).

2. *A.* Trace the sun, sun path, hills, mast and sail from the picture on pages 82 and 83 and cut them out in the materials suggested in the list above. *B.* Trace the boat but extend it 2 inches (5 cm) deeper than the part you can see in the picture. (The lower portion is hidden under the waves and the boat must be sufficiently deep to hold the fishermen.) Cut out one piece in black felt and one in thin cardboard. Thirteen pieces not counting the sun path and fish.

3. *Base:* Cover the board with purple material, folding it over to the back and sticking or lacing firmly in place.

4. *Background:* Stick the two "hills" pieces, the sun and sun path in place.

5. *The Sail:* The sail is rolled and tied up out of the way because the fishermen are busy casting their nets. Paint the gaff and mast black and ink in the draping marks on the sail. Tie brown wool round each "fold", knotting it at the back and cutting off ends except the centre fold at the mast and that at each end where long ends are needed for "rigging". Stick the mast and sail in place.

6. *Boat:* Stick cardboard backing to felt piece, then stick boat in place, attaching by a strip about ½ inch (1 cm) wide along bottom and sides only. Push the top edge out, away from board, to form a "pocket". Stretch the three sets of rigging downwards and stick to purple base inside top edge of boat.

7. *Wave Trough:* Find a shallow cardboard box or lid about 10 inches (25 cm) long and cut a strip off one edge (leaving the sides on box on the two short ends and one long edge.)

Make the cut edge uneven and wavy (look at picture for rough shape and size). Cover this piece with purple material to match background by folding it over and sticking at back and leaving two "flaps" at each side (Fig. 63 A and B). Stick the "trough" to picture spreading adhesive sparingly along bottom edge and on flaps at sides.

8. *Waves:* Look at picture and cut one or two curved pieces of purple material. Stick to board, overlapping each other and covering bottom half of boat and flaps on wave trough. Place picture on one side.

9. *Fishermen:* These are made like Jonah in the companion volume on Old Testament toys, but I have taken the work one step further and inserted pipe cleaners into their limbs so that the little men will bend and take up various positions.
Place the body pieces together in pairs and oversew all round outside edge, pushing doubled pieces of pipe cleaner into each limb as you work

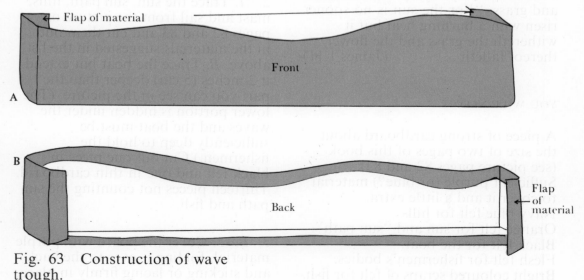

Fig. 63 Construction of wave trough.

and stuffing head and body firmly with a little cotton wool or kapok, pushing into place with a cocktail stick or toothpick (Fig. 64).

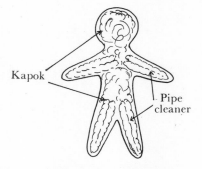

Fig. 64   Stuffing the Fishermen.

10. *Tunics:* Wrap a tiny scrap of rough weave, brightly-coloured material round each body and oversew in place (Fig. 65).

Fig. 65   Making the tunic.

11. *Hair:* Stitch a tiny bundle of wool in place for a beard also one to back and one to top of head for hair (as shown for Sower, Fig. 53, but in this case stitch instead of sticking). Trim beard and hair and arrange neatly with the help of a little adhesive. Mark eyes and brows with black ballpoint pen. I made three fishermen—Simon, James and John— (St. Luke 5.4 and 10) but your boat will probably hold five or more. Place them on one side.

12. *Fish:* Stick a felt shape to each side of a cardboard foundation, at the same time inserting three steel pins—one at the tip of the head and one at each point of tail, so that the pin heads only are exposed (Fig. 66). Mark eyes, mouth, fins and tails with black ballpoint pen and make as many fish in as many colours as you wish. Put fish into wave trough formed by box. " . . . they inclosed a great multitude of fishes and their net brake . . ." (St. Luke 5.6).

Fig. 66   Position of pins inside fish.

13. *Net:* Cut a small piece of netting and sew a tiny magnet to the centre of one long edge. Stick one end over end of boat (look at picture). Put the fishermen into boat and bend the arm of one of them to hold the other end of net.

14. *Playing with your Toy:* Unhook net from fisherman's arm and dipping net into "wave trough" see how many fish you can catch on the magnet.

"And they beckoned their partners, which were in the other ship, that they should come and help them. And they came and filled both ships, so that they began to sink."

(St. Luke 5.7)

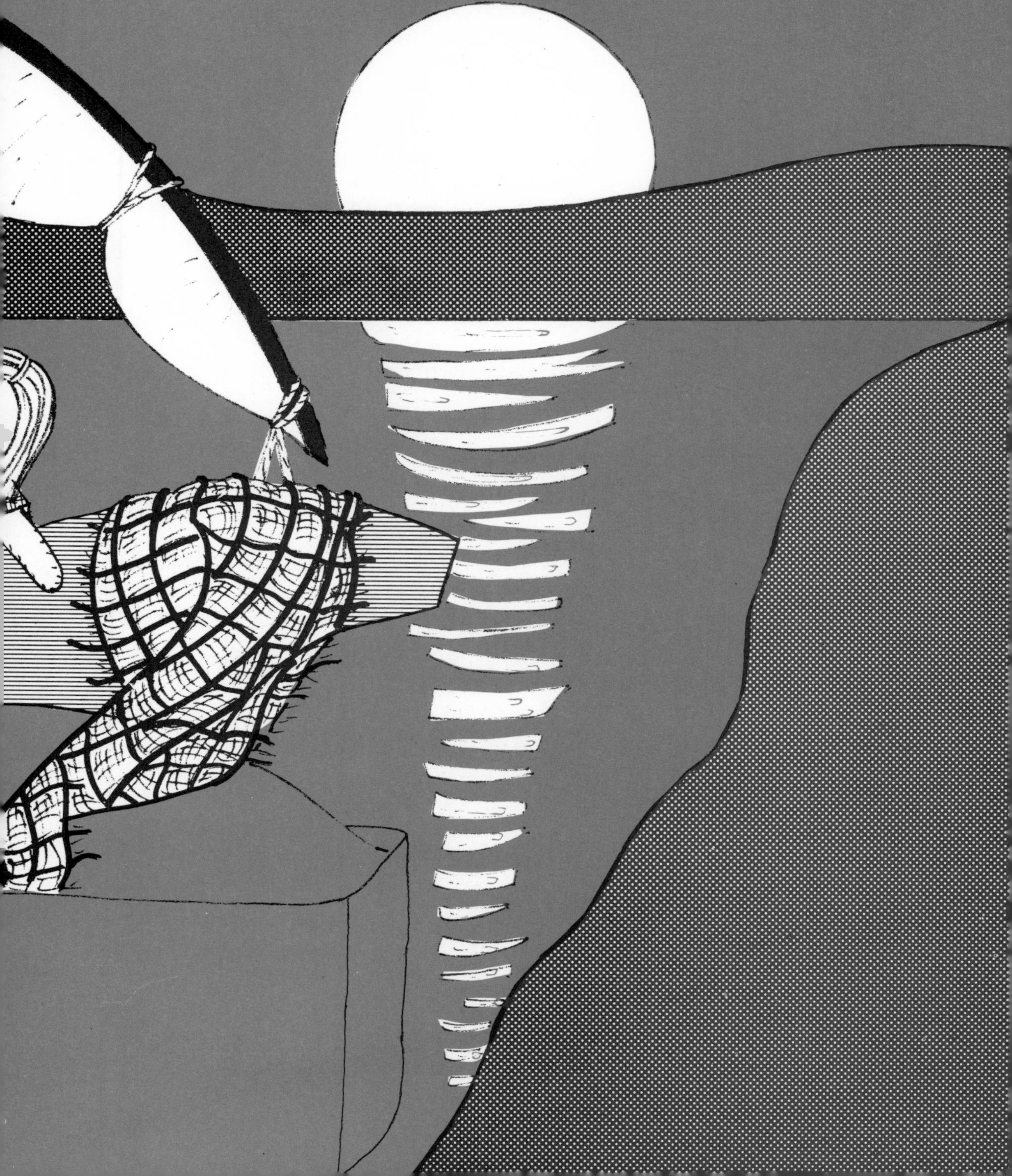

A Host of Angels

"The Angel said unto them "Fear not: for behold I bring you good tidings of great joy which shall be to all people."   (St. Luke 2.10)

Perhaps you would like an angel or even a host of them to go with the Nativity figures at the beginning of this book or to use with other characters you have made from this or the companion volume. Having worked through the books you should have no trouble making a very varied selection in assorted sizes and shapes. Those on the opposite page are just a few basic ideas to start you off.

Patterns for wings and halos are on page 95.

Bodies are containers covered with white felt or other suitable material (see page 8, No. 2; and page 32, No. 2, Figs 1 and 9).

Heads are "balls" of flesh stockinette or other suitable material (see page 40 No. 8, Fig. 15).

Hair Styles may be varied and are of yellow wool, stuck or stitched in place. (See pages 41, 68 Fig. 18 and 53).

Faces and Wing Markings are drawn with ballpoint pens; red nose and mouth. Black eyes and markings.

Sleeves: Where used are stuck in place round the three "outside" edges—like a "patch", covering ends of hands/arms.

Hands/Arms are half lolly (popsicle) sticks covered with flesh-coloured felt for Angels 1, 2 and 3 (see page 9, No. 4 Fig. 2) and flesh felt shapes cut as for the Apostles (pattern page 92) for No. 4—reduced in size for numbers 5, 6 and 7. These last four are stuck in place in a praying attitude as for Bartholomew, page 31.

Weight Smartie Tubes with a pebble to stop them overbalancing.

Angel 1: Salt tin. Head approx. 1½ inches (4 cm) diameter. Sleeve pattern as for Joseph (page 89).

Angel 2: Salt container cut to 7 inches (18 cm) (see page 9, No. 3). Head approx. 1½ inches (4 cm) diameter. Sleeve pattern as for Mary (page 89). Reverse wings.

Angel 3: Sloping yoghurt container or reversed cream carton. Head approx. 1½ inches (4 cm). Fold of robe as for Mary (page 13 No. 8 and page 9, No. 7). (Pattern page 90).

Angel 4: Smartie tube. Head approx. 1 inch (2·5 cm) diameter. Sleeves cut as for Oriental King (pattern page 89) but smaller to fit this figure.

Angel 5: Two thirds Smartie tube. Tiny pink felt feet stuck to base. Head approx. ¾ inch (2 cm).

Angel 6: One-third Smartie tube. Feet as 5. Hair—yellow wool loops stitched round front of head. Head as 5.

Angel 7: One-third Smartie tube. Wings reversed. Fold of robe as for

Mary (page 13, No. 8 and page 9, No. 7). (Pattern page 90). Cut out very small to fit this figure. Head as 5.

"And suddenly there was with the angel a multitude of the heavenly host praising God and saying "Glory to God in the highest and on earth peace and goodwill to all men."
(St. Luke 2.13, 14)

CENTURION

"There was a certain man in Caesarea called Cornelius, a centurion of the band called the Italian band . . ."   (Acts 10.1)

Centurions figure prominently in the books of the New Testament—as you probably know these men each commanded a "Century" of the Roman army. You can probably guess where we get our modern word "sentry". This Centurion looks very friendly and is quick and easy to make.

YOU WILL NEED

Four Smartie tubes (see page 6) for the limbs.
A cardboard tube from a toilet roll for the body.
Sufficient fawn felt to cover these.
A piece of old nylon stocking and a little stuffing for head.
One cup from an egg carton and some silver foil for helmet and "armour".
A few brass paper fasteners for "studs".
Scraps of material for tunic and scarf and braid for "crest".
A twig for staff.

HOW TO MAKE HIM

1. *Limbs and Body:* Cut the Smartie tubes as Fig. 67 and cover these and the toilet roll with fawn or flesh felt, either stitching as Fig. 1 A page 8, No. 2, or sticking as Fig. 9 page 32, No. 2. Stick and stitch legs to base and arms to sides of body in a marching position—look at picture.

2. *Neck:* Make a little roll of felt

Fig. 67   Shape of Smartie tube limbs.

about $\frac{3}{4}$ inch (2 cm) wide (Fig. 68). Stick and stitch to top of body.

Fig. 68   Rolling felt for neck.

3. *Head:* Make as for devil, page 40 No. 8, Fig. 15, having it about the size of a golf ball so that it will fit into a cup of an egg carton. Embroider a little piece of hair, also eyes, brows, nose and mouth (Fig. 69). Stitch to top of neck.

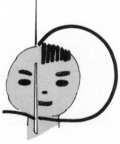

Fig. 69   Embroidering the hair.

4. *Helmet:* Cut one cup from a fibre egg carton as in Fig. 70 A. Cover by pressing foil well over the outside (B). Decorate with paper fastener "studs". Bend top forwards (C) and stick a piece of stiff braid or trimming in place for crest. Look at picture. Put on head. (Stick in place if you wish.)

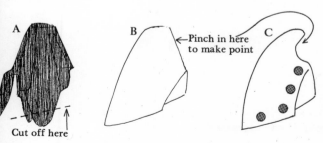

Fig. 70   Cutting and covering egg carton for helmet.

5. *Top of Tunic:* Lay a strip of material over each shoulder to form an epaulette (look at picture). Stick in place at waist.

6. *Kilt:* Pleat or gather a piece of material round the waist, stitching firmly in place.

7. *Scarf:* This was known as the centurion's "focale" and was worn to prevent the armour chafing his skin, so wrap a scrap of material round the neck and stitch to front of body.

8. *Armour:* Make two thick squares of foil about 2½ inches × 2½ inches (6·5 cm × 6·5 cm) by folding several pieces together, so that it is very strong. Decorate with brass paper fasteners. Stick two doubled or trebled strips of foil over shoulders, then stick one prepared square to the front and one to the back of the body.

9. *Staff:* Sew a piece of strong twig to one hand—a centurion always carried a stout vine staff as a symbol of rank. This will enable the figure to stand up firmly.

———

If you want to add more details, make your centurion a cardboard sword, decorate him with gilt trimmings and make him a long, purple cloak.

———

" . . . the soldiers' counsel was to kill the prisoners lest any of them should swim out and escape, but the centurion, willing to save Paul, kept them from their purpose . . ."

(Acts 27.42, 43)

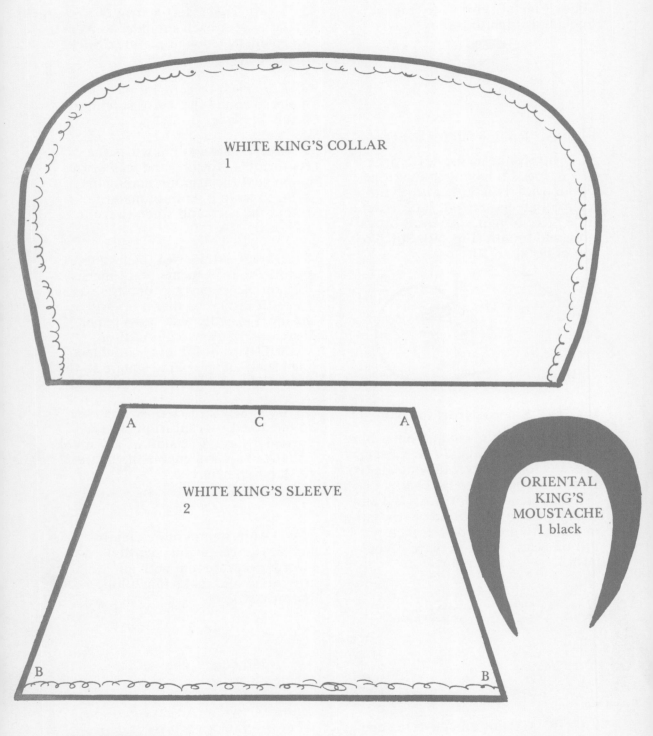

WHITE KING'S COLLAR
1

A C A

WHITE KING'S SLEEVE
2

ORIENTAL
KING'S
MOUSTACHE
1 black

B B

THE NATIVITY

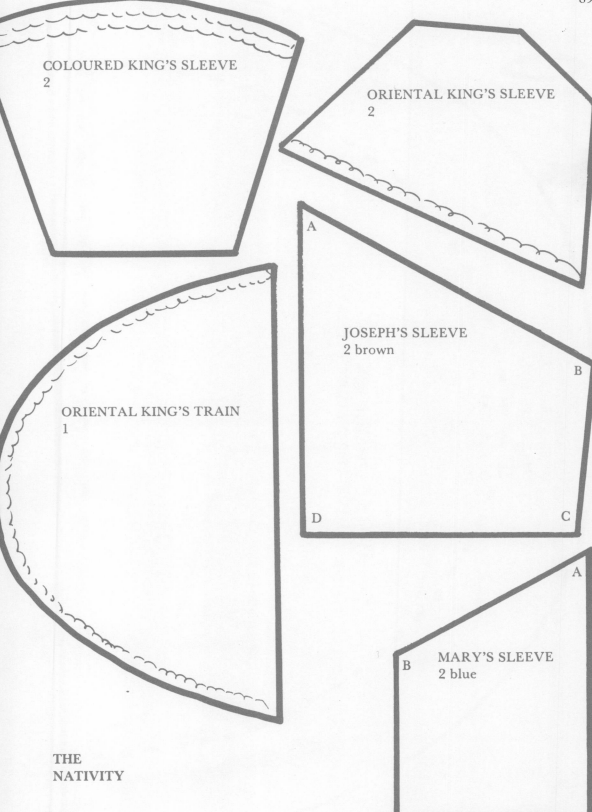

COLOURED KING'S SLEEVE
2

ORIENTAL KING'S SLEEVE
2

ORIENTAL KING'S TRAIN
1

JOSEPH'S SLEEVE
2 brown

A

B

D

C

A

B

MARY'S SLEEVE
2 blue

THE
NATIVITY

ORIENTAL KING'S EYE

2 white

MARY'S VEIL 1 blue

T

X

FOLD OF ROBE
FOR MARY AND JOSEPH 1 blue

O

W

Y

V

Y

W

THE NATIVITY

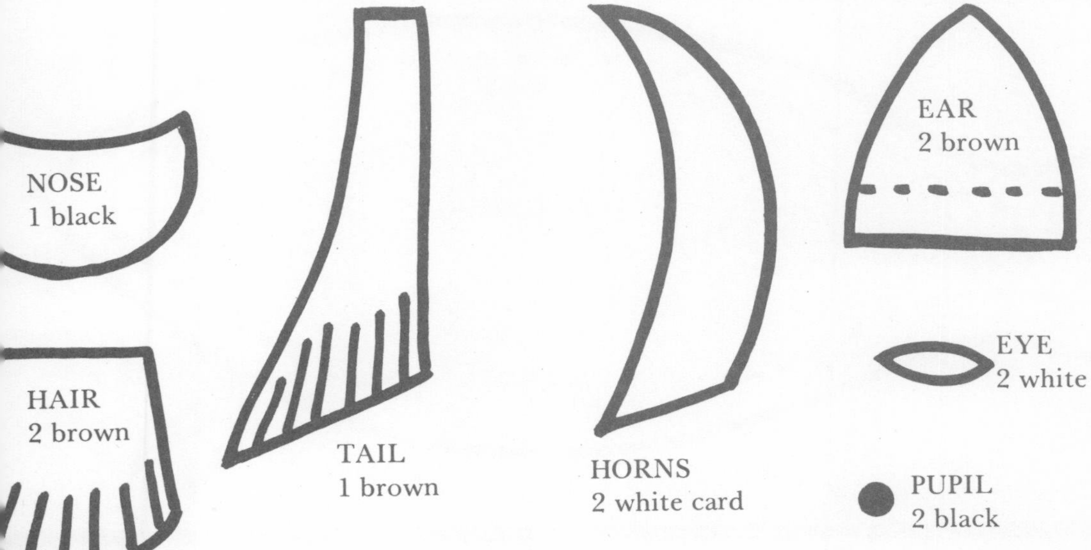

NOSE
1 black

HAIR
2 brown

TAIL
1 brown

HORNS
2 white card

EAR
2 brown

EYE
2 white

PUPIL
2 black

THE OX

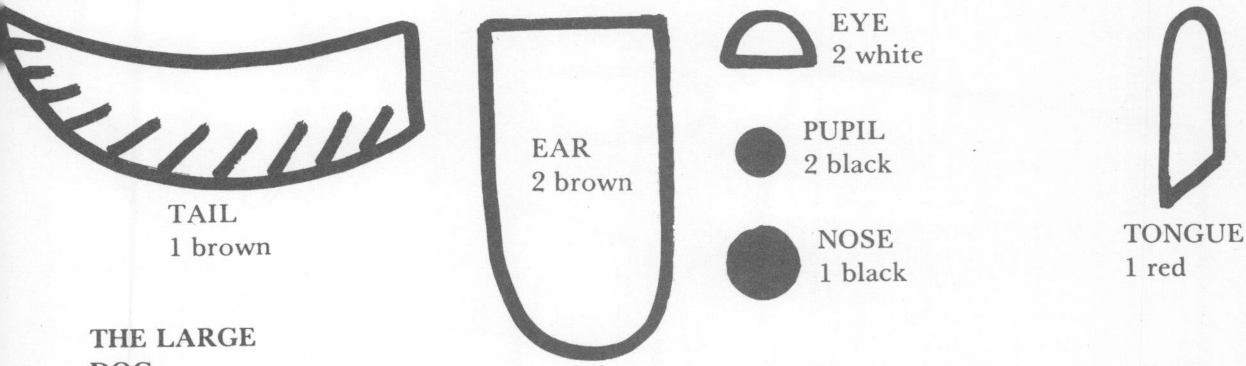

TAIL
1 brown

EAR
2 brown

EYE
2 white

PUPIL
2 black

NOSE
1 black

TONGUE
1 red

THE LARGE
DOG

TONGUE
1 red

THE
SMALL
DOG

1st WING
4 fawn

TAIL
4 fawn
2 card

EAR
2 brown

2nd WING
4 fawn

BEAK 2 fawn

PUPIL
2 black
EYE
2 white

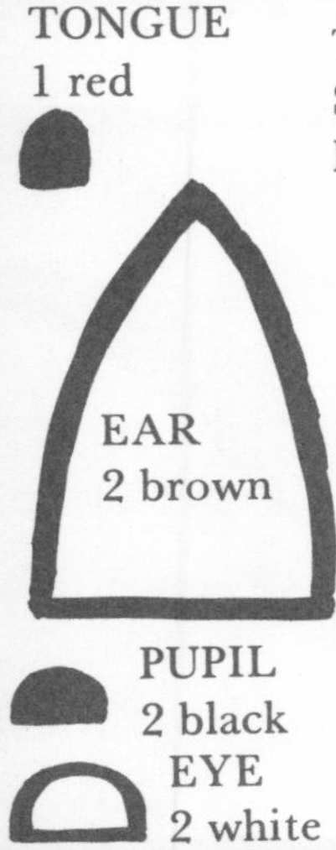

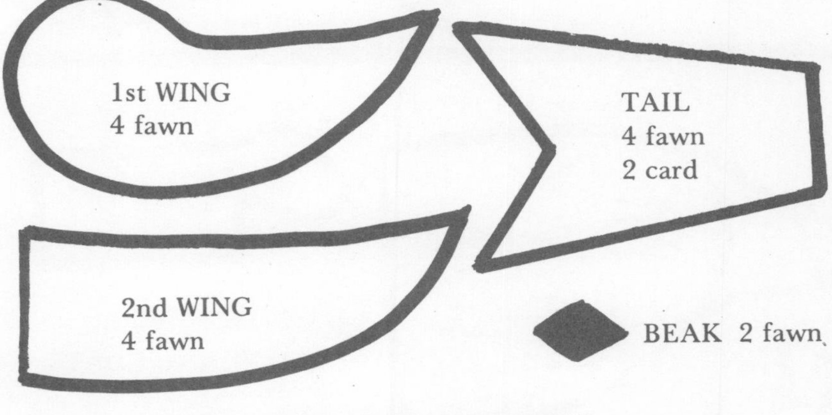

TWO SPARROWS SOLD FOR A FARTHING

92

FISH PINCUSHION 2

opening

DOUBLE HANDS 8

JAMES'S FISH
(card)

BARTHOLOMEW'S
LEAF

GALILEE

CANA

SINGLE
HANDS 8

JOHN'S SLEEVE
back 1

JOHN'S
SLEEVE
front 1

SIMON'S MAP
1 in card

THE APOSTLES

SHEPHERD 1 card

GOAT card

BIRDS

SHEEP AND GOATS

6 black
3 card

SHEEP'S
HEAD card

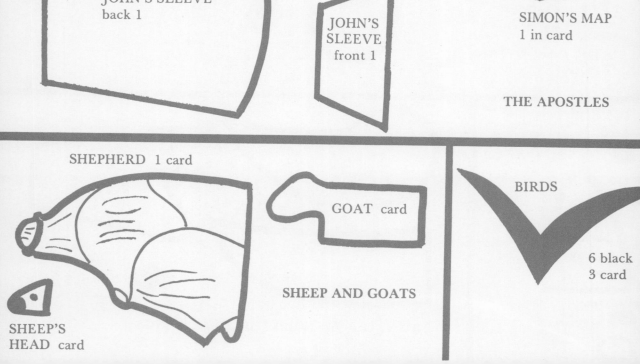
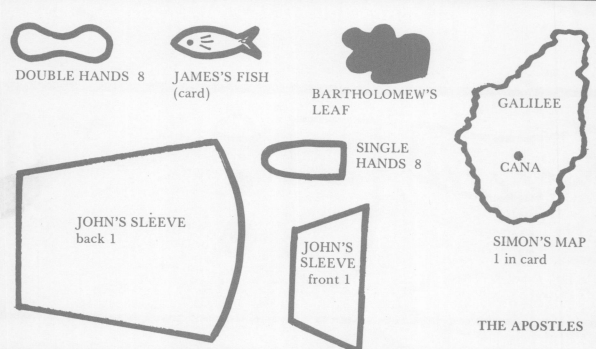

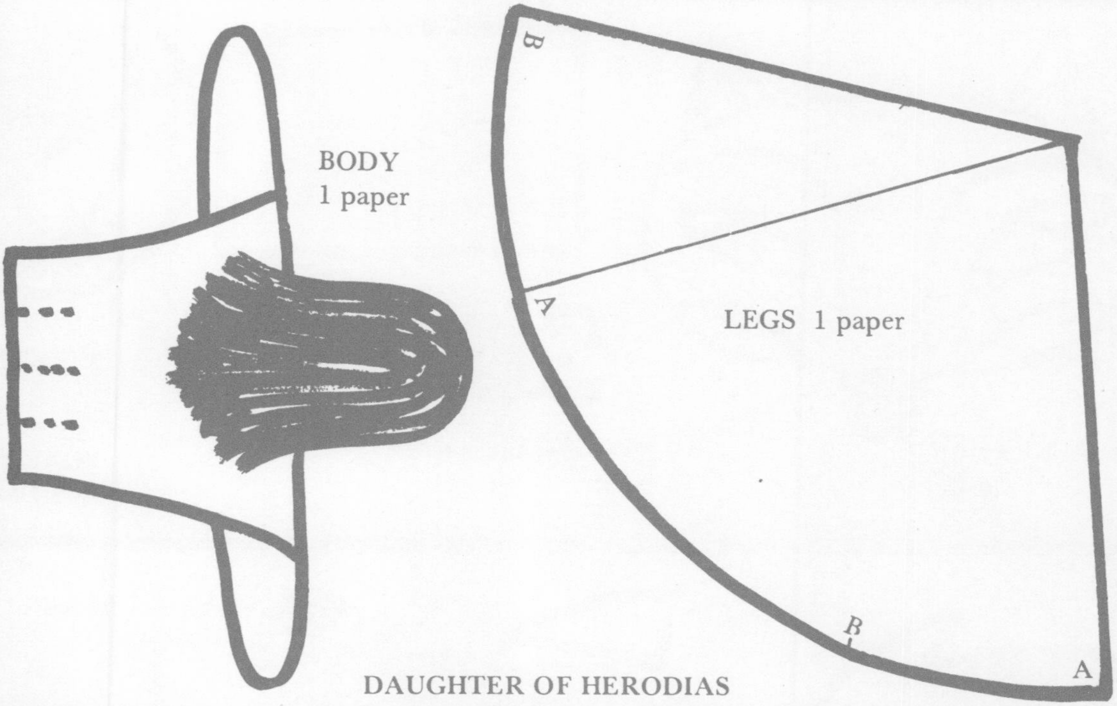

BODY
1 paper

LEGS 1 paper

B

A

B

A

DAUGHTER OF HERODIAS

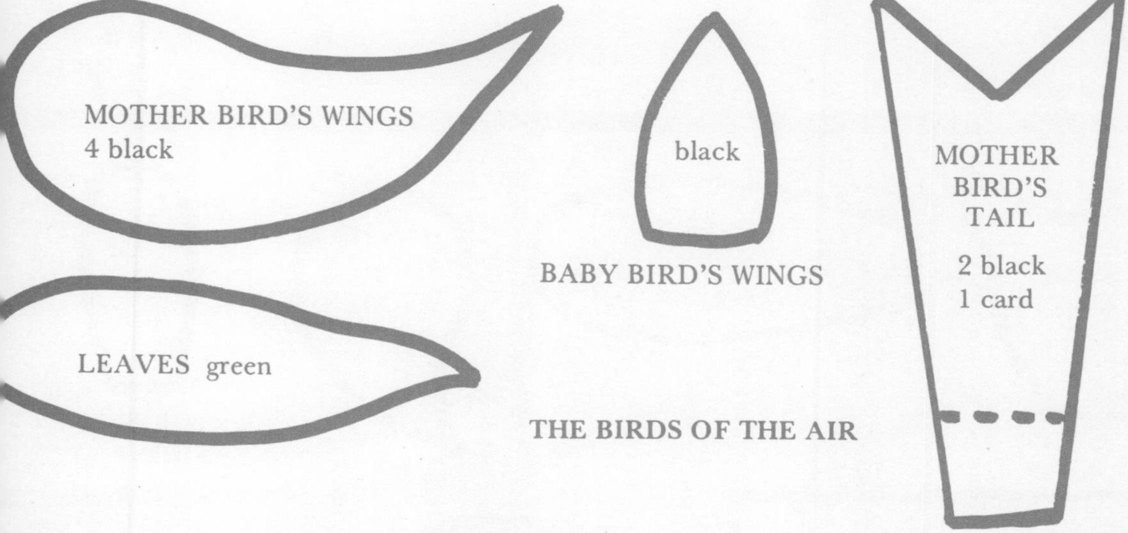

MOTHER BIRD'S WINGS
4 black

black

MOTHER
BIRD'S
TAIL

2 black
1 card

BABY BIRD'S WINGS

LEAVES green

THE BIRDS OF THE AIR

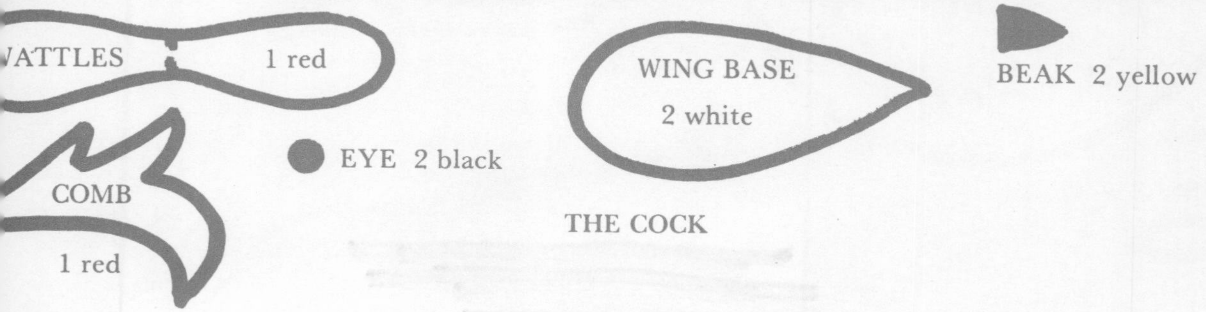

WATTLES   1 red

EYE 2 black

WING BASE

2 white

BEAK 2 yellow

COMB

1 red

THE COCK

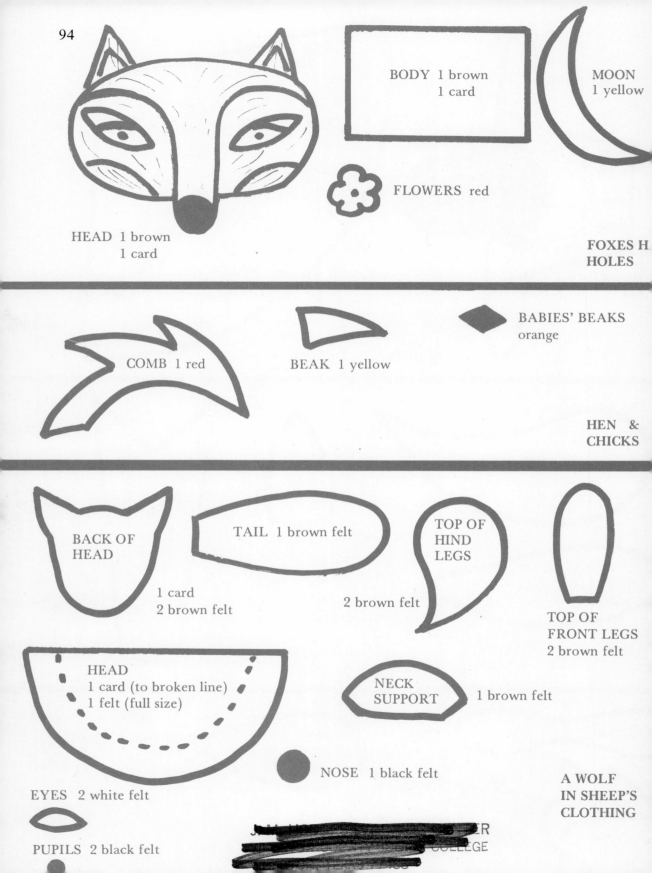

HEAD 1 brown
1 card

BODY 1 brown
1 card

MOON
1 yellow

FLOWERS red

FOXES H
HOLES

COMB 1 red

BEAK 1 yellow

BABIES' BEAKS
orange

HEN & CHICKS

BACK OF
HEAD

TAIL 1 brown felt

TOP OF
HIND
LEGS

TOP OF
FRONT LEGS
2 brown felt

1 card
2 brown felt

2 brown felt

HEAD
1 card (to broken line)
1 felt (full size)

NECK
SUPPORT

1 brown felt

NOSE 1 black felt

EYES 2 white felt

A WOLF
IN SHEEP'S
CLOTHING

PUPILS 2 black felt

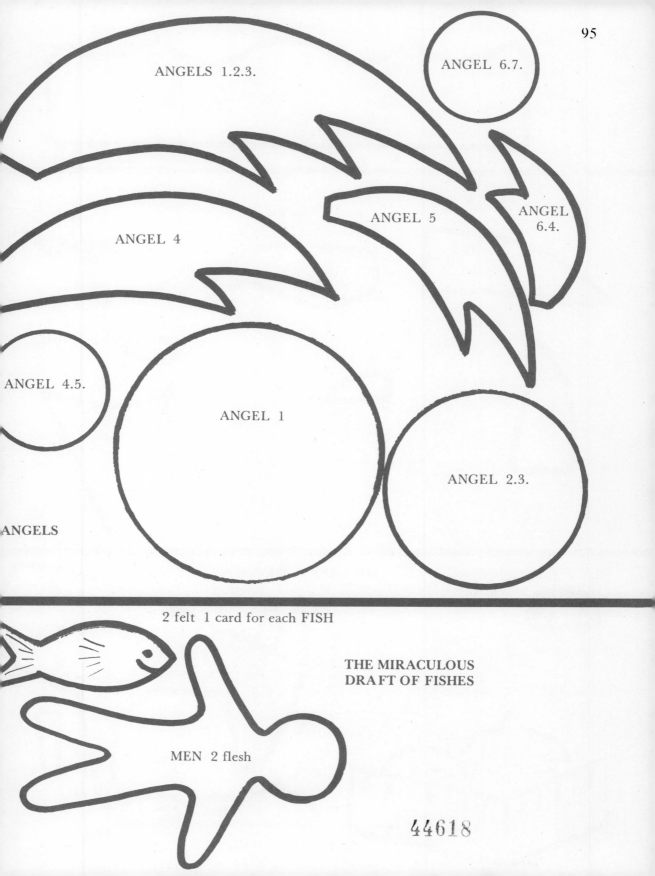

ANGELS 1.2.3.

ANGEL 6.7.

ANGEL 4

ANGEL 5

ANGEL 6.4.

ANGEL 4.5.

ANGEL 1

ANGEL 2.3.

ANGELS

2 felt 1 card for each FISH

THE MIRACULOUS DRAFT OF FISHES

MEN 2 flesh

44618

WHITE KING'S CROWN 1

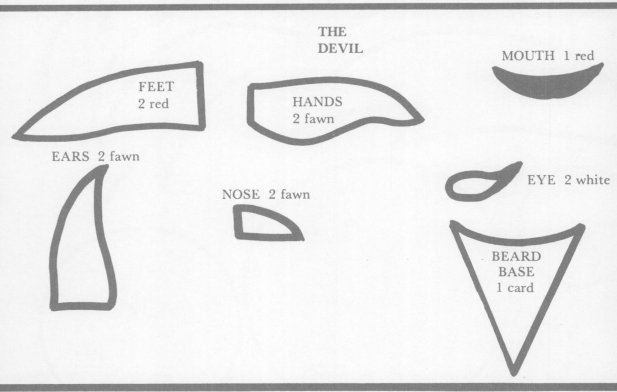

THE DEVIL

MOUTH 1 red

FEET 2 red

HANDS 2 fawn

EARS 2 fawn

EYE 2 white

NOSE 2 fawn

BEARD BASE 1 card

THIEF'S HEAD 3 flesh

THE GOOD SAMARITAN

ASS 1 grey

JERUSALEM 1 white

THI ARM 2 fle

JERICHO 1 white